BREAKING FINANCIAL BARRIERS:

Messages for Financial Empowerment

William D. Watley

D1111688

All scripture quotations are taken from either the New
Revised Standard Version (NRSV) or the King James
Version (KJV) of the Bible.

For copies contact:

Rev. Dr. William D. Watley, Senior Pastor
St. James A.M.E. Church
588 Dr. Martin Luther King, Jr. Blvd.
Newark, New Jersey 07102
(973) 622-1344, Ext. 111 (office)
(973) 622-6912 (fax)
www.williamdwatley.com

New Seasons Press, 2006
Printed in the USA
ISBN 0-9772409-2-4

DEDICATION

CHARLES ALEXANDER MAXELL, III

JULY 9, 2006

GRANDSON

May you live long and prosper God's way.
May you bring as much joy to your parents' life as
your parents have brought to mine.
Above all,
May your life glorify God in what you become and
with what you acquire.

TABLE OF CONTENTS

INTRODUCTION

Financial bondage and barriers can block us from achieving our greatest potential; they can short-circuit our quest for a healthy, wholesome and peace-full life, and they can negatively impact our desire to serve God with our whole heart. The principles and guidelines in this book have been tried by a number of persons who have followed them diligently. Their testimony is that they work and are worthy of emulation. My hope and prayer is that these guidelines and principles will also enable you to live and walk in God's vision of financial freedom and prosperity for your life, as I have found them to be effective in my own life.

I am grateful to Almighty God for revealing these principles to me and I am thankful that in the people of St. James A.M.E. Church in the City of Newark, New Jersey I have found committed core of faithful followers who have a passion for financial freedom and openness to new visions.

Thank you Dr. Raquel St. Clair, Executive Minister, for critique and standing in the administrative gap so that writing projects such as this one can be finished on time.

As usual I am deeply indebted to Mrs. Carolyn Scavella for both her editing expertise as well as her ability to format and prepare manuscripts for publications. The breadth of your talents, continue to amaze those of us who are privileged to be beneficiaries of your competence and commitment.

Thank you, Mrs. Muriel Watley. You have always supported my writing ministry and never complained when it took too much of my time.

BREAKING FINANCIAL BARRIERS

You Must Follow The Rules

TEXT: EXODUS 16: 13-30

When God gives us a vision we can rest assured that the vision will not be an easy one. Visions are mental pictures that God shows us that grip our hearts and are radically different from our present situation or reality. Changing our present reality or situation will not be easy. Visions by their very nature are growth oriented; they challenge us to grow. As such then, visions that come from God are borne out of prayer. They come to those who seek God's face or abide in the presence of God. They are consistent with the word of God because God is not going to tell us to do anything that contradicts the word of God. Visions will be a blessing to others since we are called to serve others. And fourth, visions are so great that we can only achieve them with and through God so that when we achieve them we must give the glory to God. Whenever there are great visions there will also be great barriers to overcome in achieving them. The greater the vision, the greater, and more numerous the barriers to be overcome. If we question why things are so hard for us, the reason is that the vision is great. If the vision were small the barriers would be small. In this life the devil, the enemy not only of God but of God's vision for our lives will not allow any great visions to be birthed without also creating barriers to be dealt with.

To achieve vision then we must be prepared not simply to face and or overcome but to destroy the barriers that come against us. If we simply overcome them, those barriers are still present to rise against us again. Our goal in life should not be to simply overcome barriers, we must seek to destroy or break them. As we pursue God's vision for our lives we will face all kinds of barriers: fear, our faith, believing, as we should or believing the right things. Sometimes friends and families will be barriers because they do not see what God has shown us or because they have their own vision for our lives. We will face the barriers of focus or staying fixed on our purpose. And for a number of us finance is a major barrier or even a stronghold that must be broken or destroyed before we can reach where God is trying to stretch us.

I am convinced that a number of us do not pursue the visions that God has for us and that a number of us tend to be so squeamish about giving and about money in general, not because we are bad people or because we intentionally want to be in rebellion against the vision or word of God. Many of our problems with obedience to either the word of God when it comes to giving or obedience to vision center around the fact that we just do not see how we can afford to pursue what God shows us, or how we can afford to give as the word of God instructs us. Sometimes God will show us things that are so big and outlandish, and sometimes what God asks appears to involve so much money that when we look at what we have to work with financially, we just cannot see how some things can happen or how we can afford to do what the word of God requires or asks. When we think about how we are just barely making it financially, when we look at how far we are in debt, we just feel like throwing up our hands and saying, "Forget it!" or, "you must be kidding."

We have a heart for the Lord. We have the anointing of God upon our lives. Some of us even feel the calling of God to certain ministries, missions, jobs, careers and tasks. We are grateful to the Lord for everything that God has done and have powerful testimonies of how far the Lord has brought us. We love to worship God and we don't mind serving the Lord or rendering service to the church. We respect and are willing to submit to the spiritual authority that God has established over and in our lives. We may even be versant in one or more spiritual gifts and have the fruit of the Spirit growing in our lives. We may even have a measure of faith. After all we would not even be members of the church or attending church if we did not have some faith. Our faith

7

may be strong or struggling, or searching, but we would not be in the church of God without some measure of faith. Some of us have demonstrated our faith as we have trusted God to heal our sick bodies, deliver us from habits and addictions, and defied demonic and human enemies who have attacked us from time to time. We have demonstrated our faith as we have put loved ones in the hands of God and as we ourselves have dared to get back up and continue believing God for certain things after we have been knocked down or after we have fallen down.

Yet with all that we have come through and been through, as much as we have trusted God in other areas in our lives, finances and money, the giving of it, the lack of it, the fear of it, not knowing how to handle it or not being able to imagine having enough of it to do what God has shown us, remains a major barrier and stronghold for many of us. I can not tell you how many times I have heard church people say, "That's too much money" or "we can't afford that," or "That's too expensive," after they have heard about a great vision. 1 cannot tell you how many times I have heard church people ask, "Where are we going to get that kind of money?" after they have heard about a great vision. What gets me is that I have seen these same people get all emotional as they have sung, "Be not dismayed what'er betide, God will take care of you," or "I'm going to trust in the Lord till I die," or "The Lord will make a way somehow," or "Hold to God's unchanging hand." Many times I have just heard these same people quote Paul's statement about God supplying all of their needs according to his riches in glory in Christ Jesus our Lord, or our sufficiency being in God. Many times I have just heard these same people testify about how God helped them pay their bills and made a way out of no way for them.

Yet while we know all of this and believe all of this, finances and money still challenge our faith. That is I strongly believe that having overcome so many others things like sickness, addiction, guilt, shame, fear, bitterness, divorce, heartache, bereavement, rejection and joblessness, money is still the last great stronghold for a number of us. After having come through and after having overcome so much, a number of us still have trouble-trusting God in money matters. We still lose sleep over money. We still worry about having enough money. We still become very sensitive and uptight about money. We still struggle to manage money. We still seem to be just a little short of having enough so that our money worries and woes will be forever solved. For others of us money is still a mystery. It is still one of the great enigmas of life and consequently we regard people who seem to have it in abundance as being a breed apart from the rest of us. We look upon them as especially smart or we hold them in some kind of awe.

I would submit to you the proposition that if we are to break the financial barriers that discourage or stop us from pursuing God's vision for our lives we must follow certain rules. The text is a demonstration of this truth. In the text, the children of Israel were faced with the challenge of how they were going to survive as they pursued God's vision for their lives. God's vision for their lives included a land of their own and as they pursued that vision they faced a number of challenges. One challenge they had faced and broken was the effort of their former slave masters to recapture and enslave them again. They had reached the banks of the Red Sea when their former slave masters reached them to take them back into captivity. However God had cut a path of dry land through the sea and had allowed the children of Israel to cross over. When the pursuing enemy tried to cross over the same path that the people of God had come over, the waters of the sea overtook them and they were drowned. The people of God had rejoiced and gave great thanks for their victory. However soon thereafter they faced the challenge of not having enough food to continue the journey. When their provisions ran short they began to complain and panic. They cried to Moses, "If only we had died by the hand of the Lord in the land of Egypt, when we sat by the fleshpots and ate our fill of bread; for you have brought us out into this wilderness to kill this whole assembly with hunger."

What is so interesting about the complaint of the people of God in Exodus 16 is that in the previous chapter, they had danced before the Lord in thanksgiving as they praised God for victory over those who desired to turn take them back into captivity in chapter 14. Also in chapter 15 the bitterness of the water in the wilderness had been sweetened for them to drink and God had led them to twelve springs of water. However when they reached this new crisis they panicked and started talking about slavery in Egypt, which was the vision that others had for them being preferable to the vision of new land and a new life that God had for them. I seriously doubt that the children of Israel had left Egypt without any provisions at all. The situation was simply that whatever provisions they had brought with them from Egypt was insufficient to carry them to the vision that God had for them. And when their provisions proved insufficient they panicked and began talking about death in Egypt being preferable to their present journey towards God's vision.

Let us never forget that whatever preparation we make will never be sufficient to take us all of the way to the vision that God has for us. The journey will always be longer than we expected. There will always be situations that we had not thought about or prepared for that will further drain us of whatever supply we had brought to carry us through. However when our resources run out on the journey, don't panic. Remember what God has already brought you through. That is the first rule of breaking financial barriers. Don't panic; remember what God has already brought you through. If God's power was able to deliver his children from over 400 years of slavery then God's power is certainly able to take care of the physical needs of his children. If God's power was able to take care of the armies of Egypt then God can certainly take care of the physical needs of his children. If God's power was able to clear a path through the sea and hold the waters back while the children of Israel crossed over, and then released them when their enemies pursued them, then God is able to take care of the physical needs of his children. After all, all they needed was bread and what is bread to a God who grows all of the grain in the world.

If God has taken care of us thus far, surely God is able to take care of our financial needs. If God has delivered us from every snare and trap that the enemy has set, surely God is able to provide us with dollars. If God has helped us conquer our habits and our guilt, surely God is able to provide some cash. If God has given us whatever we have needed, then surely God will help us get a grant. If God has lifted us, surely God will help us get a loan. If God has made a way out of no way in every other situation and perform miracles, surely God is able to provide money. After all it's only money. Since God owns everything and grows everything in the world, then God is able to provide for our needs. When God shows you a vision, don't panic at the price tag; just remember how God has already provided.

When the people complained, God answered in two ways. That evening God answered with quails that covered the ground, and the children of Israel who moments before thought that they were perishing, ate their fill. The next morning when they arose they saw a layer of dew around the camp. When the dew lifted they saw a fine flaky substance on the ground. They asked Moses, "What is it?" Moses called it manna or heavenly bread. When we are faced with financial barriers rule number two is, God is able to bless us in ways that we understand and in ways that we don't understand. The children of Israel were familiar with the quails, but they had never seen manna before. Manna was a new way of providing for them, that they had never seen and did not understand.

Many times when we see visions we limit God to ways and people that we understand and have experienced before. However new financial challenges mean that God is able to bless us in ways that we have not seen before and do not understand. When we are faced with financial challenges God will not only send friends and resources that we know about, but God will also bring people into our lives and resources into our lives, that we have not seen before, have not experienced before, and we will not understand why they chose to bless us as they have. When we are faced with financial challenges God will not only open familiar doors, God will also open up doors that we do not know about and do not know how they were opened to us. When we are faced with financial challenges God will not only bless us with means that we know about and understand, but with miracles that we do not understand.

By the fact that God uses both familiar and unfamiliar means to bless us; points out rule number three, which is that even when we are in the wilderness, since we are on our way to the vision that God has for us, God will not send us anywhere where God's provision cannot keep and take care of us. Are you on your way to the place of God's vision and you find yourself in the wilderness short of what you need to survive and keep going? Perhaps the enemies have pursued you and even though they have been defeated, you are facing new challenges and your resources have run out. Or perhaps your enemies are still around to undermine, threaten and to do everything they can to stop you, and your resources are in short supply. Whatever your situation is, this much I know, God will not send you where God's provision cannot keep you. If you feel that you are too far to turn back to Egypt and still too far away from Canaan to make it on what you have and you don't know what to do. Don't panic, remember where the Lord has already brought you from and what God has already done in your life. Know that God is able to bless you in familiar and unfamiliar ways. And know that God will not bring you where God's provision cannot keep you. God has not brought you this far to leave you. God has not brought you this far to let the devil have the final victory. God has not brought this far so that you will be a laughing stock to those who want to see you fail. God has not brought you this far for you to perish in the wilderness. God's grace is still sufficient and God's strength is still made perfect in weakness. God will not bring you where God's provision cannot keep you.

The children of Israel were told how much manna to gather. They were told to gather about an omer or about two quarts per household. Some gathered more and some gathered less. However when they measured how much they had gathered, everyone's container had the same two quarts of manna. Rule number four is that God knows how much each of us needs to live according to the vision God has for us and God will place in our lives the sufficiency and the abundance according to the vision that God has for us. So many times we don't know how to gather manna. Some of us are afraid to gather what God wills for us. We don't believe that God desires that we should have all of the manna that God told us we could. We don't believe the vision for prosperity or abundance that God showed us. We operate with a survival mentality that says as long as we have enough to make it then we are satisfied. Some of us have been working all of our lives just surviving from check to check and month to month.

Even though there is a whole field of manna in front of us and God has told us to gather two quarts, we only gather a pint. We work just enough to have a pint. We save just enough to have a pint. We have 'a good enough mentality' that says, "A pint was good enough for my mother it is good enough for me." Or, "a pint is good enough we don't want to get greedy." Or, "For generations all my family had was a pint. We never owned but have always rented because ownership required a quart and we have contented ourselves with just a pint." Or, we chose to live on a certain side of town because that is what we can afford with the pint we have gathered. All the while God is saying to us, "I had willed, I had envisioned two quarts for you, and here you are praising me for pints. I had willed two quarts for you and here you are packed up and ready to go to heaven because all you have is a pint."

Let me point out that our being willing to settle for a pint not only applies to finances; it also applies to God. God says to us, "I want you to have two quarts of me. I want you to seek my face and abide in my presence so that you can have two quarts of my anointing, two quarts of my power, and two quarts of my favor. However we do only enough to gather a pint. We worship God enough to have just a pint. We pray to God enough to have just a pint. We read enough Bible to have just a pint, and never gather enough to have the kind of relationship that God wants us to have with God. We fail to realize that God has restricted the devil to one quart. If we gathered the two quarts of relationship that God willed for us we would not have to fear the devil. However because we only gathered a pint, we will always be vulnerable to being overpowered by the devil.

While some of us are gathering less than what God wills for us, others of us are always looking in the manna buckets of others and are trying to compete with others for manna. We are not content with the two quarts that God has willed for us. According to our self-serving, shortsighted vision, we want more than what somebody else has. Even though what God has willed is sufficient provision and abundance for our lives, we want more than what others have and so we are not able to enjoy our two quarts because we are trying to get more manna than somebody else. Or, we are trying to keep up with the manna that is in the bucket of the Joneses. However we fail to realize that God is a great equalizer and that at the end of the day, everybody ends up with the same six feet of earth. The Bible reminds us that we brought nothing into this world and we will carry nothing out. God has a vision of manna for your life, and there is no shortage of it so gather according to God's vision and don't worry about the manna buckets of others.

The people were told how much manna to gather and then they were told to consume it on the same day. However some did not listen to the word of instruction and ended up losing what they had kept in disobedience because what they kept bred worms and spoiled. Then the people were told to gather twice as much on the sixth day because they were to rest on the seventh day. There would be no manna on the Sabbath Day and because there would be no manna provided on the Sabbath Day what they kept over on the second day would not spoil as it did on other days. There were still those who went out to the field to gather manna and found none. God gives instructions about the preservation and management of manna and if we would break the manna barrier we must always obey the word of God. That is the fifth rule; always obey the word of God. Even if the word does not make sense to us, we are not wiser than God, just obey it. If God knows how to bless then God knows how to manage what God has blessed us to have. Obey the word. We will never break the financial barriers that threaten to block God's vision for our lives unless we obey the word. Our victory in financial matters like our victory in life is found in our obedience to the word.

Somebody asked Jesus, "Why are we filling these jars with water when what we need is wine?" However when they obeyed the word they discovered that he is able to bring the best out of the ordinary. Somebody asked the Lord Jesus what was He going to do with two fish and five barley loaves among so many. Jesus told them to organize the people in groups of fifty and then he thanked the Lord for what He had and told the disciples to distribute it. When they obeyed the word, they discovered that the Lord is able to bring abundance where there seems to be little. Somebody asked the Lord why He was opening the tomb of Lazarus since He had been dead for four days, and by this time his body has begun to decompose. However when they obeyed the word, they discovered that Jesus really is the resurrection and the life. Somebody asked Jesus why He was returning to Jerusalem where his enemies were planning to kill him. Why didn't He just stay in Galilee where his ministry was being blessed? However when they obeyed the word they discovered that God is able to give resurrection and new glory with all power in the very place where enemies sought to destroy us.

Would you have peace today? Would you like to be able to lay down and sleep without guilt, without shame, without fear, without worry about how you are going to make it, without stressing about what enemies might say or do and without anxiety about money matters? Would you like the peace that comes from knowing that you are not in bondage to anything or anyone? Then obey the word. Jesus said, "Come to me, all you that are weary and are carrying heavy burdens, and I will give you rest. Take my yoke upon you, and learn from me; for I am gentle and humble in heart, and you will find rest for your souls. For my yoke is easy and my burden is light."

Our victory over addiction and over attacks, over bondage and over brokenness, over demons and over debt, and over finances and over foes is found in our obedience to the word of the Lord and the Lord of the word. Our victory over failure and over frustration, over lies and over loneliness, over money and over mess, and over poverty and over problems is found in our obedience to the word of the Lord and the Lord of the word. Our victory over sin and over suffering, over temptation and over trouble, over vice and over viciousness, and over worry and over welfare, is found in our obedience to the word of the Lord and to the Lord of the word.

BREAKING FINANCIAL BARRIERS

Breaking The Tradition

TEXT: NUMBERS 27: 1-7

The text focuses upon a group of women who questioned, and then challenged a long standing tradition that was not only found in Israel but in many of the eastern lands of that time period. The tradition they challenged had been set for so long, and had been ingrained in the cultural norms and minds of people for so long, that it was accepted as one of the facts of life that could not be changed. The tradition that the women in the text questioned and challenged revolved around inheritance issues, specifically regarding the ownership of land. According to the established cultural tradition of that era, women were not allowed to inherit land or much of anything else. The inheritance of a deceased male was handed down to the male children of the family, beginning with the eldest. The intelligence of a daughter, the talent or capability of a daughter, the propensity of a daughter for business or management, had nothing to do with certain decisions regarding inheritance. Certain decisions about who was to receive what, were based upon gender bias that rewarded males and automatically excluded women. To be born female during that time meant that no matter what qualifications one had there were certain opportunities that were going to be denied that had nothing to do with ability. To be born male during that time meant one had certain rights and privileges that were based exclusively upon genitals and not genius.

Some people are where they are not because they have done anything to be there or because they are smarter than others or because they have worked harder. Some people are in certain places of privilege because they are born into cultures whose norms give them favor, while others through no fault of their own, are excluded from full participation and inheritance rights. The question I want to wrestle with is, what do we do when God has given us a vision that is greater than any vision that we can have for ourselves or others can have for us, and the system or the culture, or the tradition, or the family, or the law, or the church or the job or the profession or the political system are in direct opposition to that vision? Breaking any barrier that blocks vision is never easy, particularly when those barriers are institutionalized, legalized, theologically and ecclesiastically legitimated, culturally engrained, socially accepted and educationally enforced. It is true that some of us have personal issues, weaknesses and sins that block God's vision for our lives, and I don't make any excuses for them. We can't blame all of our issues on others. However, it is also true that some of the personal baggage that we have has been handed down to us through family traditions [generational curses are real], as well as through educational and even religious institutions, through social and cultural norms that have taught and instilled low self-esteem and low ambitions.

Some of us have grown up with warped values and twisted self perceptions that instilled a poverty mindset, a welfare mentality, a get over spirit, and a personality that contents itself with mediocrity and just enough to get by, rather than striving for excellence. We look at those who have and those who do not have based upon how certain people look or their gender or their clothes or their background or the side of the tracks they come from or their physical condition or the texture of their hair or the color of their skin. We conclude that the world, as we see it, and have experience it, and the world that has been defined for us, is the way it has to be, now, henceforth and forevermore. Even though God has shown us a vision that is greater than we had for ourselves or that others had mapped out for us, we look at the traditions of poverty, ignorance, drama and craziness that has been in our families, our school systems, our churches, our neighborhoods, or our race for years, and we ask who are we to challenge them.

Who do we think we are to try to get out of poverty and build a life of assets and material abundance and financial prosperity without consumer debt, when poverty and welfare and borrowing to make ends meet, has been in our family for generations? Who do we think we are to believe that we can live debt free, when everybody we have ever known and everybody around us and the whole culture that shaped us teaches us that it is normal and even good to create debt with interest rates and carrying charges that keep us locked into financial bondage so that we can have what we want right now? Who do we think we are to move away from the old neighborhood or get away from the rest of the family when they have been living in the same four block area of town for years? Who do we think we are to believe that we can graduate from college and get graduate and post graduate degrees, when our family has always dropped out of school or been content to get a high school diploma? Who do we think we are to believe that we can own our own home or business when we come from generations of renters and people who have always worked for others? Who do we think we are to join a certain church when our families have been traditional A.M.E.'s, or Baptists, or Pentecostals, or Catholics or Presbyterians or atheistic or agnostic for years? Who do we think we are to become a believer who is anointed, Spirit filled and fire baptized, when our family, friendships, social and professional traditions don't affirm all of this Holy roller stuff?

Who do we think we are to desire to be a professional who has no great passion for marrying and having children when our family tradition and the culture says that is what makes us a whole woman or man? Who do we think we are to want to be a homemaker when we come from generations of professionals or generations of business people? Who do we think we are not to want to go into the family business when others have been preparing us and expecting us to take it over? Who do we think we are to marry someone of another race or religion when our family tradition and the norms of the culture dictate otherwise? Who do we think we are to believe we can occupy certain positions when the inheritance rights have been passed down to others who are not who we are? I will tell you who we are, we are those to whom God has given a vision that goes beyond what the traditions of family and culture tell us we must follow.

This is the story of the text. As I have already stated, according to the culture of that time, land inheritance rights were the provinces of men. However there was a man by the name of

18

Zelophedad who did not have any sons, only daughters. As a matter of fact he had five daughters whose names were Mahwah, Noah, Hogan, Micah and Torah. There was also a belief in Israel that the land was not to pass from one's family. Thus the existential situation of the daughters of Zelophedad, the way God made them, the place God put them and the talents God had given them, put them into conflict with two well established cultural traditions and laws. Law and tradition said that only males could inherit land. Law and tradition also said that the land should not pass from the family. The problem was that there were no males for Zelophedad to pass the land to. If the land was given to them as his rightful heirs then the law about males inheriting land would be set aside. If the land was not given to them because God had made them different than what the law and tradition stated, then the law concerning land passing from one's family had to be set aside.

What do you do when God made you in such a way that you don't fit the tradition or the culture? That is where a number of us are—God made us in such a way that we are at variance with the tradition or the law or the way the culture had defined us. God made us with ambition while the culture and the tradition said we are supposed to be lazy and shiftless. God made us to be anointed while the culture and tradition have said we are supposed to be addicted. God made us to be bountiful while the culture and tradition have said we are supposed to be broken. God made us to be bold while the culture and tradition have said we are to be in bondage. God made us to be conquerors while the culture and tradition have said we are supposed to be conquered. God made us with class and the culture and tradition have said we are supposed to be crass. God made us to be creative while the culture and tradition have said we are supposed to be confused.

God made us to be financially delivered while the culture and tradition have said we are supposed to be in financially in debt. God made us gifted while the culture and tradition have said we are to be in grief. God made us to be great while the culture and tradition have said we are to be in the ghetto. God made us intelligent while the culture and the tradition have said we are supposed to be ignorant. God made us to be loved while the culture and tradition have said we are supposed to be the least. God made us with laughter and the culture and tradition have said we are supposed to be languishing. God made us with potential and the culture and tradition have said we are supposed to be petty. God made us to be prosperous while the culture and the tradition have said be in poverty. God made us to be redeemed and the culture and tradition have said we are to be rejected.

God made us with substance while the culture and tradition have said we are supposed to be shallow. God made us with strength while the culture and tradition have said we are to be in stress. God made us to be saved while the culture and tradition have said we are to be in sin. God made us with self-confidence while the culture and tradition have said we are supposed to have no or little confidence. God made us with virtue and the culture and tradition have said we are supposed to be vulgar. God made us with vision and the culture and tradition have said we are supposed to think like a victim, live like a victim and talk like a victim. God made us to be workers while the culture and tradition have said we are to be on welfare. God made us with willpower while the culture and tradition have said we are made to be weak. God made us to be anointed, creative, intelligent, virtuous, and powerful and we are black or female and the culture and tradition have said qualities are supposed to belong to males or other ethnic groups because they have the rights of inheritance and privilege.

What do we do when God has made us in such a way that we find ourselves in variance with the culture and the tradition? We can live in frustration because we know that we have been gifted in ways that don't fit the paradigm or mold or tradition but we are trying to force a fit where one is not supposed to be. That is why some of us are so angry and negative. That is why some of us go through our careers or work life in jobs that are beneath us. That is why some of us continue to go from job to job, relationship to relationship and church to church. That is why some of us continue to encounter failure after failure. We are trying to force ourselves to fit into places and roles our family traditions or the culture have said are our places and we know deep within God has shown us another place and another role to occupy. Whenever we spend our lives trying to live up to the expectations of others rather than the vision that God has shown us we will probably find ourselves living below or beneath all we can be in God.

Then some of us allow others to make decisions about our lives. We let the tradition or culture define our place either because we are lazy or because we are so brainwashed that we believe everything the culture and tradition say about us, so we live lifestyles of destructive self-fulfilling prophecy. Don't believe everything the prevailing culture or the tradition says about you. Don't believe the stereotypes the culture and tradition portray about you. And whatever you do, don't believe everything the prevailing culture with its traditions of biases, say about people you know or your leadership. Sometimes we choose to go along to get along because we don't believe we can do anything about long established traditions and cultural norms.

The five daughters of Zelophedad chose not to live frustrated or to simply accept the customs of the time. They chose to question the prevailing norm and tradition of their time no matter how long established they were or how fixed they were in the minds of people. They went boldly to Moses, Eleazar the priest, the leaders and all the congregation, at the entrance of the tent meeting and said, "Our father died in the wilderness; he was not among the company of those who gathered themselves together against the Lord in the company of Korah, but he died for his own sin; and he had no sons. Why should the name of our father be taken away from his clan because he had no son? Give to us a possession among our father's brothers." Upon hearing their request, Moses brought their case before the Lord. "And the Lord spoke to Moses, saying: 'The daughters of Zelophedad are right in what they are saying; you shall indeed let them possess an inheritance among their father's brothers and pass the inheritance of their father to them.'

If we are to break the barriers and the traditions that block God's vision for our lives, financially and otherwise, there are at least three points that we can glean from the daughters of Zelophedad. First, they knew who their father was. He was not one of those who had rebelled against the leadership of Moses, which may have disqualified them to receive an inheritance. He was one of those who had left Egypt and had died on the way to Canaan because of his unbelief. However while his faith was not perfect, his imperfections did not cause him to lose his inheritance. As his children they knew that they had a right to his inheritance. They may not have known what the outcome of their plea would be, but they knew they had a right to more than what the tradition and what the culture were going to give them if they said nothing. Therefore without any guarantee they came forward to claim what was theirs based upon who their father was. If we are to break the financial and other barriers that block God's vision for our lives, we had better be clear about to whom we belong and whose child we are. We don't have to accept just any old thing the culture throws our way and we don't have to be content or try to force ourselves into traditions that have been set by our families and others.

When we know who our real Father is, who created us, who provided for us, who protected us and helped to grow us, then we know that no matter what others think or say, we have some inheritance rights. No matter what traditions stand in our way, we have inheritance rights. Therefore when traditions of exclusion stand in our way we need to claim our inheritance rights. In God's word we were promised, "The Lord will make you the head, and not the tail; you shall be only at the top, and not at the bottom—if you obey the commandments of the Lord your God (Deuteronomy 28: 13)." In God's word we were promised, "For surely I know the plans I have for you, says the Lord, plans for welfare and not for harm, to give you a future with hope (Jeremiah 29: 11)." The Lord Jesus Christ who has birthed us has promised, " I have come that you might have life and have it more abundantly (John 10: 10)." The Lord Jesus Christ who died in the wilderness of Calvary for our sins has given us inheritance rights that defy any tradition or culture, "Ask and you shall be given; seek and you shall find; knock and the doors will be open to you (Matthew 7: 7)."

When others ask why you are getting uppity, beside yourself and out of your place; when others ask you why you can't be content with the traditions that have been in place for, "lo these many years," just tell them who you belong to. When others tell you what you cannot do or dare not do, when others tell you not to fight the system but simply accept whatever crumbs the system throws your way and be grateful, tell them to whom you belong. When others think they can destroy you if you go beyond what they have determined is acceptable for you, which will always be much less than what they think belongs to them, tell them who you are. You are one of Zelophedad's children. You are a child of God. You belong to the Lord Jesus. You have the very presence of God, abiding within you and around you, known as the Holy Spirit. You have a song that not even the angels can sing, "Redeemed; redeemed, you've been redeemed."

First, Zelophedad's daughters knew their inheritance rights because they knew who their father was. God had placed Moses in their midst, one of his servants with authority who knew how to handle their petition. When Moses heard their petition, he did not try to answer it himself. And neither did he take it to other humans who had as little wisdom as he had. Instead he took it to the Lord. When you belong to God then God will put people in your life, who have authority and who know how to help you out. Don't worry about your foes, when you know to whom you really belong, then God will give you favor with the right people who have as much power if not more than the people who are working against you. When foes close a door in your face, God will send friends to open up another door. When foes knock you down, God will send friends to lift you up. When foes lie on you, God will send friends to speak up for you. I once heard President Clinton say that the weak will inherit the earth but you need somebody to first write them into the will. When traditions and customs and viciousness and jealousy try to keep you out of God's will and vision for your life, the Lord will send somebody else to write you in. Therefore when you find yourself being written out or kept out, don't panic just know the Lord is sending somebody else to put your name in a place where others can't reach you. Somebody can testify God is faithful and God will not allow those who belong to him to be written out of his will, no matter what tradition says.

The daughter's of Zelophedad could question the tradition that had no place for them to inherit anything because they knew who their father was. They knew to whom they belonged. Secondly, God had placed someone in their lives who had authority and who knew what to do with their situation. Third, they could question the tradition which tried to set limits on their lives to receive an inheritance because God had the last word. After Moses presented their case to the Lord, the Lord spoke and when the Lord spoke no matter what the tradition had been, no matter what others may have thought, no matter how many thought the daughters of Zelophedad had gotten out of their place—when the Lord spoke the case was settled, the issue was resolved, the inheritance was granted because the Lord had the last word.

That is why we can go up against barriers and traditions that seem immovable and impossible to overcome—the Lord has the last word. That is why we do not fear those who would destroy our names, our reputations, our careers, or our lives—the Lord has the last word. That is why we do not sell our souls to anyone or bow to what little power they think they have over us—the Lord has the last word. Some of us know that the Lord has the last word. Some of us know what it is to receive dismal news about our health and to be given dire diagnoses but we are still here because—the Lord had the last word. Some of us know what it is for people to trash us and think that they have the victory over us, but the Lord has the last word.

Noah preached for over a hundred years about a flood and looked like a fool when he gathered two of every species of animal and nobody believed him. But one day the rain started falling and Noah's faith was justified because the Lord has the last word. If you are standing on the word, vision and promise of God keep on standing even though nobody believes you and even though you may look foolish—the Lord has not spoken yet and He will have the last word. If Moses and the children of Israel coming through the Red Sea prove anything, if Hainan's futile plot to destroy Modecai and the Jewish people prove anything, if Elijah's victory over the 400 priests of Baal and the 450 prophets of the pagan deity Ashtaroth prove anything, it is this truth—the Lord will have the last word. If the presence of the fourth man in the fiery furnace with Shadrach, Meshach and Abedngo prove anything, if Daniel's victory over the lions proves anything it is this, the Lord will have the last word.

If the signing of the Emancipation Proclamation by a racist Abraham Lincoln whose main concern was saving the union, but could not save it unless he freed black slaves proves anything, it is this—the Lord has the last word. If the signing of the bill naming a holiday after Dr. Martin Luther King, Jr. by a reluctant, recalcitrant, resistant, and racist Ronald Regan after Dr. King had been scandalized by the FBI, betrayed by his good friend Ralph Abernathy, rejected by the administration of Lyndon Johnson because of Dr. King's prophetic stand on the Vietnam War, misunderstood by a number of we blacks, forsaken by a number of white liberals and shot down by racists in Memphis, Tennessee proves anything, it is this—the Lord has the last word.

We are who we are as followers of the Lord Jesus Christ because the Lord has the last word. They hung him high, they stretched him wide, they buried him, sealed the tomb, and posted a guard to make sure that nobody stole the body. But early Sunday morning nobody broke in, but the power of God broke out. The power of our risen and triumphant Christ broke out and he rose to stoop no more with all power in his hands. The Lord really does have the last word. I don't know where you are in your life. You may be agonizing in Gethsemane. You may be at Calvary where you feel more lonely and forsaken than you have ever felt before. Your enemies may be gloating because they think that they have the victory over you. Some of those you thought were your friends may no longer have faith in you. But no matter how dark it looks at the moment, remember God has not spoken yet and God will have the last word. God's word will be a word of resurrection, a word of vindication, a word of healing, a word of power, a word of faithfulness, a word of love, a word of forgiveness, word of cleansing and a word of freedom.

The Lord has the last word. Addiction does not have the last word; the Lord has the last word. Sickness does not have the last word; the Lord has the last word. Suffering does not have the last word; the Lord has the last word. Evil and demons do not have the last word; the Lord has the last word. Death does not have the last word; the Lord has the last word. Financial bondage does not have the last word; the Lord has the last word. The media does not have the last word; the Lord has the last word. That is why we can break traditions and cultures that want to deny us our inheritance, the Lord has the last word. No matter what today looks like, your future is in the hands of the Lord who has the last word.

BREAKING FINANCIAL BARRIERS

Overcoming The Midas Problem

TEXT: MARKS: 24-34

Money or financial barriers are for a number of persons, the major obstacles that stop us from pursuing God's vision for our lives. Financial barriers consist of money issues that we struggle with that prevent us from either seeing or believing or pursuing Gods' will and vision for our lives. For some of us money and finances are barriers to pursuing God's vision because we have problems managing them. For some of us money and finances are barriers to pursuing God's vision because we are so much in debt that we cannot conceive of our ever getting our heads above water so that we can breathe free again. For others of us money and finances have become barriers in our pursuit of God's vision because we cannot conceive of the prosperity that God has shown us or we cannot see where the resources are coming from so that the vision can happen. For still others of us money and finances have become barriers to the pursuit of God's vision because we have attached too much importance to them. Many of us believe that the key to our happiness and to well-being and power is money. I lift before you the bold proposition that many of us need to be delivered from our idolization of money and the expectation that money, like the old tonics and lineaments, is a cure for whatever ails us and that it holds the key to power and even self-esteem.

When we think about the circumstances in which some of us were raised we can understand how and why money became the key for so much self esteem and power. If we were raised poor, so much of what we could not have was due to a lack of money. We had love, we had support, we had prayer, we had good examples, but what we did not have was money. When we asked for certain things or when we asked to go certain places and do certain things we were turned down not because we were not loved, or because the decision makers in our lives did not want us to have certain things, they just didn't have the money. It just seemed like the things we wanted the most were always things that we could not afford. Consequently money became the missing link to our happiness and fulfillment. Since we had almost everything else we wanted; we came to believe that if we just had more money then life would be complete. Ask any of us now what would make us most happy, we would tell you that we would like to be able to buy what we want without always having to worry about the price or the budget. If we grew up with money we recognized early that money was key to our being able to enjoy the lifestyle that brought so much joy to our lives. Thus, we came to believe that the key to our continued happiness is found in our money. Whether we are rich or poor, anytime we start believing that money holds the key to our happiness and well being, then money has us in a stronghold and can be a barrier to our receiving everything that God envisions for us.

I want to be clear that I am not trying to assert that having or wanting more money is a bad thing. I agree with Sophie Tucker who said, "I've been rich and I've been poor. Rich is better." Even though I am not rich, neither am I trying to go back to some of the poverty that I have known. I am not trying to romanticize any supposedly good old days when there was no food in the refrigerator and nothing to drink but water and I was struggling from paycheck to paycheck just to make ends meet and praying hard that nothing major happened in between. Middle class and upper middle class are better than poverty. Ninety-nine percent of the people I know, worldly people and saints alike, like money and like the things that money can buy. I have discovered that the same people who criticize us for admitting that we like money and what it can buy, like it too. They are either working hard trying to get more of it themselves or they are jealous of somebody who has more of it or they are worrying because they might not have enough of it or they are pinching pennies and trying to hold on to as much of it as they can or they are fantasizing about what they would do if they had more of it, or they are playing the lottery or the numbers.

I am not downplaying the importance of money. I just want us to understand that if we do not have a correct understanding of money and what it can and cannot do, then money and finance can become barriers to the vision that God has for us and can create as much of a problem for us as it was for old King Midas. Like a number of you, when I was in grade school and learned Greek mythology, one of the stories that I remember was that of King Midas, the ruler of ancient Phrygia. According to the story, one day Midas gave assistance to Dionysus, the Greek god of revelry, and as a reward, Midas was granted one wish. Midas had a fascination for gold and so he requested that everything he touched be turned into gold. Midas was granted his wish and touched a tree and it turned to gold. Then he touched a horse and it turned to gold. In a matter of minutes he was becoming the richest man in the world.

However his golden touch started giving him trouble when he became hungry. When he sat down at the table to eat, the meat that he touched also became gold, as did the wine that he desired to drink. When he could not do something as simple as satisfy his hunger, Midas discovered that the touch that was supposed to bring so much happiness also brought headaches, which soon lead to heartbreak. Midas' daughter did not know about his touch, consequently when she hugged him, she too became solid gold. Midas went back to Dionysus and begged him take his golden touch away from. Dionysus sent Midas to the source of the Pactolus River where he was to bathe so that he could be restored to normal. Midas took his daughter with him and they were both changed to their previous state. It was only after he lost his touch that he became happy again. The touch that was supposed to bring riches brought revulsion. The touch that was supposed to bring delight brought death. The touch that was supposed to bring merriment brought misery. The touch that was supposed to bring smiles brought sorrow. The touch that was supposed to bring power brought problems. The touch that was supposed to bring blessings brought a curse.

Sometimes we hear the expression 'Midas touch' used as a compliment. It means that someone has a knack for making money. And I dare say that some of us have at times wished we had that kind of gift, where everything we touched turned to gold or was financially lucrative. However when we look at the story, the Midas touch was not a good thing for the person after whom it was named. He discovered that what he thought made him happy ended up making his life a living hell. Some of us already have had experiences with things that were supposed to bring happiness and brought us hell. We have already had experiences with Midas touches that went wrong and brought the wrong things into our lives. Some of us are living in situations, working in situations and trying to be delivered from situations that seemed like pure gold at first and have turned out to be grime.

Midas' problem was that he put too much value in gold. He thought that the more gold he had the happier he would be. However when he had the opportunity to get all of the gold that he could possibly reach, he discovered that the sum total of life could not be measured by the amount of gold that he owned. When he was robbed of the joy of eating food and touching his own daughter bringing death to that once gave him joy, he discovered that life was greater than the gold standard. Never make money the center of your life. Never make money the source of your self-esteem. Many years ago the Hunt Brothers, who were the sons of the famous H.L. Hunt, the legendary oil baron and tycoon of Texas, were brought before a congressional committee for attempting to monopolize the silver market. They tried to own so much silver that they alone could determine the value of silver. When they were questioned, one of them was asked how much they were worth. One of the brothers replied, "We don't know how much we are worth." The congressman could not believe his ears and asked again, "You have so much money that you don't know how much you are worth?" The Hunt brother replied, "If a man can tell you how much he is worth then he can't be worth very much." The congressman replied, "Well, that's the truth."

For years I struggled with the answer given by the Hunt brother and the response of the congressman. I do not know exactly what the Hunt brother meant by his answer, but the question was asked with regard to financial worth. Frankly it does not take me very long to sit down with a pencil and paper and figure up my financial worth. I concluded that since my financial worth could be added up so easily, I must not be worth very much. I must confess that there have been times when I did not feel that I was as successful or as productive as others because I did not have the money they do. Even now, if I am not careful, I have to struggle to keep from feeling less than others if I cannot financially afford what others can. Even now I have to struggle with not feeling like a failure if I do not have the kind of financial bottom line that I think others have or that I know they have.

I have a sneaking suspicion that I am not the only one who has to wrestle with problems of poor self-esteem and feelings of inferiority that come from ones financial assessment. As long as we have financial inferiority or anxiety, then we will not be free to receive whatever vision God has for us because we will be measuring ourselves by the gold standard, or we will be measuring the vision by the gold standard, or we will be measuring God's love for us by the gold standard, or we will be measuring the worth of the vision by the gold standard. Whenever the gold standard becomes the ruling standard for our lives, our self-esteem, our sense of self-worth or our productivity or our sense of being loved or blessed, then whether we have money or not, money and finances have us in captivity and in bondage. They...money and finances... have the vision that God has for us in captivity. They have our faith in captivity. They have our minds, our hearts and our spirits in captivity. They have our love and our very lives in captivity.

The touch of Midas limited him. It imprisoned him in a very small world. However, when we read the text, we discover that there is another touch that brings value beyond the gold standard, that brings healing and self-esteem, that brings life and wholeness. If we do not have that touch we will always have a Midas problem... putting value in the wrong things and expecting self-esteem and power to come from the wrong sources. If we do not have that touch we will always have a Midas problem, looking for fruitfulness and fulfillment, love and life, happiness and hope, peace and prosperity in all of the wrong places. If we do not have that touch we will always have a Midas problem, not be able to understand the limitations and the uses of money. If we do not have that touch we will always have a Midas problem, being so focused on the gold standard and becoming so limited that we forget about the other things and the people in our lives that give us joy.

If we do not have that touch we will always have a Midas problem, having plenty but still being poor and miserable. If we do not have that touch we will always have a Midas problem, not being able to see beyond or see farther than the gold standard. If we do not have that touch we will always have a Midas problem, bringing death rather than deliverance to our lives as well as those who are around us. If we do not have that touch we will always have a Midas problem, not having wholeness and healing for situations that we have been laboring with a long time. Do you have a Midas problem?

In the text, the person who initiated the right touch was totally different from Midas. Midas was a powerful king; she was a vulnerable woman. Midas was healthy and physically well, she was sick and weak. Midas only dealt with the curse of his touch for a short while, but she had been sick for twelve long years. Midas was rich with gold, she was poor because she had spent all she had trying to get well but only grew worse. We know the name of Midas but we do not even know the name of the woman in the text. Midas then was a person of importance; the woman in the text was so anonymous that she easily became lost in the crowd. When I look at her situation I am reminded that any of us can have the touch that brings God's vision of healing and wholeness, deliverance and salvation to our lives. Our situation may be like the woman in the text of worsening rather than getting better. That is where some of us are today. We are trying to get free from financial bondage, but things seem to be getting worse rather than better. We praying as hard as we can, we are doing everything that we know to do, and things seem to be getting worse instead of better.

What do we do when everything we touch turns to frustration rather than success? Like the woman in the text, we refuse to accept our condition as permanent. No matter how long we have been laboring with something or someone, no matter how many times we have tried and failed, we continue to believe that there is a touch that will bring life. There is a touch that will bring healing. There is a touch that will set us free from the limitations, the anxieties, and the insecurities that come when we live and bow down before the gold standard. There is a touch that will release us to live in the vision that God has for our lives. There is a touch that will help us stand up straight with confidence rather than slouch with poor self-esteem and stoop with fear. There is a touch that will set us free from what we think is the irresistible pull of the flesh. There is a touch that will set us free from the bondage of habits and the bondage of the past. There is a touch that will bring healing to our hurts and our rejection. Therefore, where we are is where we happen to be not where we have to be. Our financial and other situations are not fixed; they are fixable, if we have the right touch.

The woman refused to accept her situation as permanent and so she did not let anything or anyone prevent her from reaching out to Jesus. She did not let the failures of other physicians or her disappointment with other physicians stop her from trying to reach Jesus. Have you been disappointed by other people? Have those whom you thought would be the ones to love you, or help you, or teach you or lead you, or heal you, or encourage you to do the right thing, let you down? Have others made promises that they did not or could not keep, and now you are tempted to stop trusting or stop believing or stop being faithful or stop trying to live right or do the right thing? Have people that you have loved or trusted or believed in or had faith in treated your love, trust, affection and good will as pearls before swine? Don't let your disappointment with others stop you from reaching out to Jesus.

Are you still surrounded by all kinds of obstacles and barriers and people that could prevent you from breaking loose from the confines and bondage of the gold standard if you allow them to have their way? Are you still surrounded by those who are active hindrances to your efforts to be free from the Midas problem? Now that you are close to breaking loose and being healed, now that you are close to victory and success, do you find a lot of last minute hurdles and hindrances that could discourage you enough to turn you around if you let them? Does there seem no end to the crowd of obstacles that keep blocking your reaching the vision of what you know that God has for you? Does there seem to be no end to those unexpected bills and unplanned for financial obligations that keep popping up out of the blue now that you have made a decision to be healed of your hemorrhaging financial condition? Some of us have been living under the tyranny and living as victims of the gold standard for so long that we are hemorrhaging. We are bleeding to death. God's visions for us and our dreams of living in peace and fulfillment are hemorrhaging. Our self-confidence and our faith are bleeding to death. Our heart is bleeding to death.

We think what we need is a Midas touch, but what we need is the right touch. And what is the right touch? The right touch is the one that reaches out in faith to Jesus. The right touch is the one that reaches out with determination to Jesus. The right touch is the one that reaches out with heartfelt need to Jesus. The right touch is one that reaches out with everything that we have to Jesus. There is only one person who can heal you and deliver you and help you to stand up straight and walk in the vision that God has for you and his name is Jesus. And don't you dare let anyone or anything stand in the way of your reaching Jesus who has the power that you need for deliverance. Only when we reach out to him will the bleeding in our lives, and in our families, that has been there for generations, stop.

The touch to Jesus is the right touch because when we reach out to Him something happens to us and in Him. Something happens between us, and at that moment, when it happens, nobody may know about it or can understand or explain it. But the two of us, Jesus and us, know that something special has happened between His heart and our heart, between His soul and our souls, between His mind and our minds, between His abundance and our needs. He stops and says, "Some body touched me." The crowd around us may not understand but we know that something has taken place between Jesus and us. You wonder why some people praise God like they do. You wonder why some people can't keep their seats in church. Those of us who are onlookers may not understand. But those who praise Him with such reckless abandon, those who have such unrestrained and irrepressible joy know, and Jesus knows that something has happened between the two of them.

Something flows from Him and something dries up in us. Acceptance flows from Him and anger dries up in us. Bounty flows from Him and bitterness dries up in us. Breakthrough flows from Him and bondage dries up in us. Delight flows from Him and depression dries up in us. Deliverance flows from Him and demons dry up in us. Excellence flows from Him and excuses dry up in us. Faith flows from Him and fear dries up in us. Grace flows from Him and guilt dries up in us. Healing flows from Him and hurt dries up in us. Love flows from Him and loneliness dries up in us. Redemption flows from Him and rebellion dries up in us. Salvation flows from Him and shame dries up in us. Tenderness flows from Him and turmoil dries up in us. Willpower flows from Him and weakness dries up in us.

When Jesus spoke up, the woman came forward to confess both her touch and her healing. Jesus told her, "Daughter, your faith has made you well; go in peace, and be healed of your disease." When she touched Him he touched her with a word of peace and healing. The same Jesus who spoke to the woman has a word of healing, release and freedom for those us who have been allowing the gold standard, money and financial barriers to block God's vision of wholeness for our lives.

I invite you, as the reader, to now bow your head and pray:: "Lord Jesus I confess that I have a Midas problem. I have been allowing financial issues to limit me and block your vision for my life. Lord Jesus I pray that you would heal me of my financial issues or any other issues that hold me back from living, as you desire me to live. I confess O Lord Jesus that I am bleeding to death. My heart is bleeding. O Lord Jesus only you can stop the bleeding. Stop the bleeding right now and heal me and help me to walk in the victory and the freedom that you desire for me. Speak a word of healing and hope to my hurt and my helplessness. Thank you Lord for restoring me and thank you Lord for the new life that I will begin right now in you and through you. In your name do I offer this prayer and in your name do I claim victory and healing, Amen."

The Lord has a word of healing for you and if you meant this prayer and are not saved you can be healed and delivered right now.

BREAKING FINANCIAL BARRIERS

What Kind Of Investment Are You?

TEXT: MATTHEW 25:14-30 (24-30)

A very interesting aspect of this parable is that the servant with the one talent was condemned for doing what many of us fail to do. He was also condemned for not doing what too many of us do. As a matter of fact most of us ought to be grateful that we were not in the parable because when we think about the way that a number of us live and manage not our resources, the punishment that the third servant received would be light compared to what we would receive if we were in the parable. To understand my assertion let us look at this familiar story again.

To begin with, we must have a correct understanding or definition of the word *talent*. In this day and culture when we use the word talent, we usually mean a natural ability or special creative aptitude such as singing, or playing an instrument, or cooking or speaking or having great athletic skill. Whenever someone performs well we say they have great talent. Often, this meaning of the word talent has been used when we have heard sermons preached with such topics as "Use It Or Loss It". However, in this parable the word talent has another meaning. The word talent also refers to a measurement of money. During the time of the Lord Jesus people not only used coins, money was also measured out by its weight. Today we speak in terms of ounces or pounds or milligrams, grams or kilograms. Some gold and silver coins are still measured by their weight such as an ounce, or half an ounce or a quarter of an ounce. The talent was a particular weight or unit or measure for money. A talent weight of silver at today's worth would be about $1500-$2000.

If we were to tell this parable in today's language we would say that a certain man going on a long trip, called three of his servants together and gave one $10,000, another $4,000 and another $2.000, according to their ability. In other words, this parable is a story about managing and handling money. It is not a story about being able to play the piano or sing, or preach or pray, but about handling and managing money. Note the basis that the man used to give a specific amount of money to his servants was not gender or sexual preference, nor the servant's education or degrees, nor the servant's physical health or looks. Ability was the basis for the distribution or money. The man did not even use his personal preferences or favorites for the decisions he made about distributing money—he used demonstrated or proven ability. In order to know their ability the man had to personally know each of the servants. He had to have observed them or had specific experiences with them that let him know what they could handle and manage. I need to remind us that the Lord knows us better than we know ourselves. The Lord has seen us manage and handle the blessings He has already bestowed upon us. The Lord has already given us money to live on and live by and the Lord has seen how we have managed or mismanaged that. As I have said before, if we have not shown that we can manage a little money, why should we expect the Lord to give us more money to mess up, waste and throw away.

If we can't manage tens and twenties but spend them as soon as we get a hold of them, why should the Lord give us fifties? And if we can't manage fifties, why should the Lord give us hundreds? And if we can't manage hundreds but immediately max out our charge cards, why should the Lord give us thousands? If we can't manage thousands, and are living from paycheck to paycheck with thousands, why should the Lord give us millions? When we have demonstrated that the more we have the more we spend, when we have shown that the more we have the more we charge and the less we give, why should the Lord give us more, when we have shown that the more we have the deeper in debt we get? Why should the Lord keep helping us dig ourselves deeper into a hole? Don't keep asking God to bless you with more money when you keep messing up the money you already have. If we want the Lord to bless us with more money then the first thing we must do is demonstrate that we have the ability to manage what we have right now.

It is only as we are faithful over a few things that we are promoted to become ruler over many. It is only in our faithfulness with little, it is only when we demonstrate that we can handle a little without going crazy and acting a fool, that we will be privileged to receive much. If we are acting crazy and acting like fools with the little we have, why should the Lord give us more to act even crazier with and bigger fools over? It is unfortunate to say but the truth is that there are many sincere love-the-Lord saints, some of whom are tithers who will never receive the financial prosperity God has envisioned for them because they do not know how to manage or handle money. We might receive some of the overflow God has for us but not all of it. I don't know about you, but I am at a point in my life when I want everything God wants me to have, and my prayer is that I don't cut off my future blessings because I don't properly manage or handle or appreciate or the blessings I already have.

In the parable, one servant received five talents; another received two and a third received one. However before we begin to feel that the servant with the one talent received the short end of the stick or that he was working at a disadvantage we should be reminded that a talent was a lot of money, equal to wages of a day laborer for fifteen years. Even though the third servant received fewer talents than the other two, he was still abundantly blessed. He still had a lot more going for him than most folks. A number of us feel that we don't do more or can't go farther because we do not have the advantage that someone else has or we do not have as much to work with as others. We feel that if we had someone else's mate or help, or parents or youth or health or education or gifts or money or opportunities, then we could do so much more with our lives. Some of us even place the blame for our low achievement on God. We feel that if God had not dealt us such a bad or disadvantaged hand we could go much father in life. Some of us need to be reminded that as poor as we are, as much as we had going against us, as little as we have in comparison to others, if we live in America, even with all of its issues, we are still much better off than most of the world.

Someone has observed that, "If you own just one Bible, you are abundantly blessed; one-third of the entire world does not have access to one. If you woke up this morning with more than health than illness, you are more blessed than the million people who will not survive this week. If you never experienced the danger of battle, the loneliness of imprisonment, the agony of torture, or the pangs of starvation, you are ahead of 500 million people in the world. If you can attend a church meeting without fear of harassment, arrest, torture, or death, you are more blessed than three billion people in the world. If you have food in the refrigerator, clothes on your back, a roof over your head, and a place to sleep, you are richer than 75 percent of this world. If you have money in the bank, in your wallet, or spare change in a dish somewhere, you are among the top eight percent of the worlds wealthy. If your parents are still alive and still married, you belong to a very rare group, even in the United States. If you were able to read the Sunday bulletin, you are more blessed than more than two billion people in the world who cannot read at all." Even with our one talent, we have started off with much more than most of the people in the world. Even with all that we claim we lack; we are still blessed and highly favored by the Lord.

After a while the three servants were called to give an account of their labors with what they had received. Let us never forget that there is a reckoning day a' coming in this life as well as the life to come. If we do not manage well whatever God has given to us, if we fail to honor God, eliminate debt, and build assets, if we fail to tithe and give according to the word of God and God's vision for our life, we will not have to wait until the sweet bye and bye to face our reckoning day. We will, as some of us already have, begin to give an account in this life of misuse and abuse of our financial resources, our body, our relationships, our friendships, our families, and anything else the Lord gives us. If we do wrong we will pay here and we will pay eternally. And if we do right we will begin to reap here and receive eternally. "For the wages of sin is death, but the free gift of God is eternal life in Christ Jesus our Lord."

When the three servants began to report, the one with the five talents said, "You gave me $10,000 and I made $10,000 more." His master told him, "Well done good and trustworthy servant; you have been trustworthy in a few things, I will put you in charge of many things; enter into the joy of your master." The servant with the two talents reported, "You gave me $4,000 and I made $4,000 more." His master told him, "Well done good and trustworthy servant; you have been trustworthy in a few things, I will put you in charge of many things; enter into the joy of your master." Note the servant with the five talents and the servant with the two talents did not receive double the reward based upon the amount of money they raised. They both received the same reward based upon their willingness to work with the blessing that they had received.

However, the servant with the one talent came in scratching his head, shuffling and looking at the ground and said, "Mr. Boss Man, Lord have mercy, I know that you are tough and demanding with high expectations. You have been known to reap where you have not sown and gathered where you did not scatter seed. I was afraid to take any risks, I was afraid to let go so that I might gain, I was afraid that I might lose the little bit that I had. I was too cheap to try to do better, so I hid what you gave me in the ground. Here is what you gave me just like you handed it over to me to do something with." To which his master replied, "You wicked and no account slave. If you knew that I was demanding why then didn't you at least invest my money with the bankers so that I could have gotten some return on what I had given you with interest? Take the talent from him and give it to the one who has ten. For to all those who have and know what to do with it, more will given and they will have greater abundance. But those who do nothing with what they have, even that will be taken away. As for this worthless, lazy, excuse making servant, throw him into the outer darkness, where there will be weeping and gnashing of teeth."

Is somebody else driving what the Lord had for you, because you did not do right by what He had given you? Is somebody else living in the house the Lord wanted you to have, because you did not do right by what He had given you? Is somebody else living happily with the person the Lord had for you, because you did not do right by what He had given to you? Does somebody have the successful career or is somebody else receiving the benefits of the job that the Lord wanted you to have, because you did not do right by what He had given you? Is somebody else enjoying the ministry the Lord wanted you to have, because you did not do right by what He had given to you? Is somebody else enjoying the wealth and prosperity the Lord wanted you to have, because you did not do right by what He had given you? I have come to a new understanding of hell. Hell is not about flames or fire and shoveling coal. I believe that hell is being forced to see all that God had for you every day, for the rest of eternity and knowing that you will never ever be able to have it. That is the kind of torture that will cause your soul to burn with remorse forever and have no peace of mind forever and ever.

This third servant was punished because he did what a number of us failed to do. He saved his money. He did not spend his talent; he did not squander it; he did not misuse it or abuse it, he at least saved it. Most of us do not do that with the consistency and regularity we should. Then, when we do save, we break into the piggy bank the first time we see the word sale, or when we decide that we need to treat ourselves to a depreciating asset like a vacation or a new outfit or a night out on the town. When one of our sorry relatives, not one of our legitimately needy relatives is going through a tough season, have their hands out and are always behind and broke, come up with another sob story, we deplete our savings. When the Lord asks us what we did with what He gave us are we going to say, "I did not do anything with it because I was afraid to take any risks?" Will we say on that day, "I sat on what you gave me because I did not want people to talk about me or accuse me of getting uppity or thinking I was better than anyone else." Will we say, "I did not do anything with what you gave me because I did not like the preacher, or nobody gave me proper recognition or because I was mad that I did not have what You gave somebody else?"

This third servant was punished because he did not do what a number of us do. At least he did not spend the master's talent and then create debt on top it. At least he brought the master his original amount intact and whole, rather than a bunch of debt he had created because he needed a release from the pressures of life, or because he was trying to keep up with the lifestyles of the other servants with the five or two talents. He did not spend the master's talent because he felt that the one talent was not much to work with anyway, or because someone sent him a charge card in the mail or because his bank increased his credit limit. He did not waste the master's talent because he had a chip on his shoulder since he only had one talent to begin with. A number of us not only fail to think about saving anything, but by using everything, we also create debt on top of what we spent. If the master was as hard on the servant who saved, what will He say to us when we tell Him, "I did not bring you any assets, but I brought you some good looking and fine wearing liabilities. I did not bring you any deliverables but I brought you some debt on an easy payment plan. I did not bring you any addition or multiplication but I brought some subtraction and division that was on sale. I did not bring even what you gave me; I am bringing less. I did not build on what you gave me, but I am bringing you bills. I did not bring what you gave me, I spent that and I brought you indebtedness."

The third servant's mistake was that he saved but did not invest. Let us never forget the Lord is expecting a return on what He has given us. The Lord does not expect us to simply hold on to what He has given us. The Lord does not expect what He has given to us to be buried and given to Him in the same condition. The Lord certainly does not expect us to come to Him in worse shape than we were when we first started out; the Lord expects some kind of return on investments. Saving is not enough; we must invest.

If we had to meet the Lord right now, how would our life read? Plus or minus? Growth or sameness? Better or worse? Making progress or just holding? At this point in our lives what return we will show the Lord based upon His investment in us and based upon His goodness to us? With all the Lord has done; with as many prayers as the Lord has answered; with as many times as the Lord has rescued us; with as many opportunities as we have had, as represented by each new day, what kind of return do we have to show the Lord?

I would submit to you that there are some simple principles for investment that will increase our portfolio or net worth. These are the same principles that the Lord follows with us. First we should start investing in what we know and understand, and build from there. The Master told the third servant, "If you do not understand Warren Buffet's system of investing; if you do not understand all that you read in the Wall Street Journal or see on the financial networks; at least could have put the money in the bank or another savings institution, as a minimum, so you could have at least earned some interest and I could have gotten some kind of return on what I had given to you." These days there are risks with everything so you might as well at least try to do better. Quit asking yourself, "What if I fail?" Start asking yourself, "What if I succeed?" Quit asking yourself, "What if I lose?" Start asking yourself, "What if I win?" Nothing beats a failure but a try. Since we are going to die anyway we might as well die trying to improve our situation. Since we are going to have to give an account for what the Lord has entrusted to our hands, we might as well show Him hands that have been busy working trying to improve our situation.

There is a story of an old washwoman who had worked all of her life trying to be a blessing to others and trying to make the most of what she had to work with. As she lay dying she said to her pastor, "I am not an educated woman, what shall I say to the Lord when I meet Him in glory?" The pastor told her, "Don't say anything Granny just show Him your hands." When we come before the judgment seat of Christ we won't have to tell Him about our faults, our sins and our weaknesses. Our enemies will be more than happy to report on all of those. We won't have to tell Him about our tears and struggles, He who has numbered the very hairs on our heads will know all about that. Just show Him your hands. Will they hold something or will they hold nothing but debt from waste and shortsighted living? Will they hold excuses or laziness because we have not tried, or fear because we did not have faith to trust the ability God has given to us to bring forth a return?

We can at least invest in what we know and understand. That is what the Lord does with us and that is why He invests in us. He knows all about us. He knows what we are made of. He knows our strengths and our weaknesses. He knows just how much we can bear. He knows the potential for great things He put in us when He created us in his very own image. He knows what we can become and that is why He died on the cross so that we could have another chance to get it right. He knows what we can do and that is why He has called each of us to some kind of ministry and service. He knows us.

In investing we must go with what we know and then try to learn something new---we must diversify—which simply means do not put all of your eggs in one basket. Spread the risk around. People who lost so much money with Tyco and Enron or even Lucent did so because they had all of their money in one place rather than spreading it around in a number of investments. That is the philosophy behind mutual funds that put a limit or a cap on how much is invested in any one stock or investment. Consequently the risk is spread around. A portfolio is a variety of stocks or investments among our holdings.

The Lord uses diversification with us. Some of us will remember when the prophet Elijah became discouraged and he went to Mount Horeb because Jezebel had threatened him. Elijah forgot about the victory the Lord had just given him at Mount Carmel and thus he ran from a threat. God asked him what he was doing there at Mount Horeb? Elijah explained to the Lord that the people had torn down his altars, killed his priests and servants and that he was the only one left and now they were seeking his life to take it away. God told him, "Get up and go back to where you ran from and I am going to give you some names of people to deal with my enemies and yours, as well as a successor for you. However you need to understand that you are not my only servant. You are not my only preacher. You are not my only singer or musician. You are not my only officer or leader. You are not my only teacher. You are not the only one in the church who is Holy Ghost filled and fire baptized. You are not the only one with sense and ideas and can think. You are not the only one that I speak to. You are not the only one who has a heart for me and does not mind giving me praise. You are not the only one with a testimony and with talent. My program does not depend just upon your money or your approval. I know how to diversity. I have seven thousand more in Israel who have not bowed their knees to Baal and whose lips have not kissed him."

The Lord even uses diversification in trying to reach and redeem us. The writer of Hebrews declared, "Long ago God spoke to our ancestors in many and various ways by the prophets, but in these last days He has spoken to us by a Son, whom He appointed heir of all things, through whom He also created the worlds."

To become a successful investor we must start with what we know and build from there. We must diversify and then we must know our risk factor. Knowing your risk factor means that you have to know your comfort level when it comes to investing. You have to know how much you can invest and still have peace and be able to sleep at night. You have to know how much you can invest without worrying. Some people have a high risk factor. In other words they can invest a lot in things with greater risks. Other people have a low risk factor. They are more cautious in how much they are willing to put into investments that carry greater risks.

I never cease to be amazed at how high a risk factor God has when it comes to us. Every time we call on God and make a promise and God hears us and gives us another chance or rescues us, God takes a risk that we will keep our word, even though we have a track record and history of breaking it. Every day the Lord sends, God takes a risk that we will not do anything or say anything that will wound God's heart, even though our track record and history is that we will continue to mess up. When God allowed Jesus Christ His only begotten, to be beaten, abused, tormented, tortured and persecuted for the sins of the world, God took a risk that giving God's best, His unspeakable gift would bring out the best in us. When Jesus went back to glory and left the future of His work and life's mission in the hands of fallible human beings who had failed Him in the past, He took a great risk. The question we need to ask ourselves is, in our giving and in our living, in our service and the things we are devoted to, are we justifying the risks that God takes in us when every morning, as the old people used to say, He "lengthens out the prickly threads of our lives and bids our golden moments to roll on a little while longer." What kind of investment are we? The question that each of us needs to ask ourselves is, "what kind of investment am I?"

The third servant thought that if he did not succeed in trying to invest and trying to do something with what he had been given, he would be punished. The punishment came not because he failed to produce but because he failed to even try. The third servant did not understand that even if He did not get it right and made some mistakes, and even if he had lost everything but had tried the best he could to improve and give the Lord some kind of return, he could have used his best and his efforts as leverage for mercy. In life you have to know about the principle of leverage. A lever helps us lift something or move something. Leverage is simply the power or weight of our influence to lift or move or get something done. When we apply for a loan, the lending agency checks our credit history and our assets, and the weight of our credit history as leverage or influence to move that lending agency to grant us the loan. When we give somebody our word or make a promise, our word acts as leverage that what we say will be done. When we ask somebody to speak to another person for us we are asking the person to use their leverage or influence with a certain person for our benefit or on our behalf.

One of the joys of being a follower of the Lord Jesus Christ is that when we give ourselves completely to him we are able to use his name and his blood as leverage. We can leverage His name against demons, against attacks and against problems, and in difficult circumstances. Whenever we say, "In the name of Jesus," that's leverage. Consequently when we are faced with challenges in life that we do not know how we can conquer, don't forget to use the leverage that belonging to the Lord Jesus gives us. When we face foes who are after us with everything they have and are determined to bring us down, before we panic and take things into our own hands, don't forget to use the leverage that belonging to the Lord Jesus gives. When we are trying to pray through and do not seem to be making any progress, before we throw up our hands in disgust, don't forget to use the leverage that belonging to Jesus gives. When we are sick and healing does not come or when we feel discouraged and the enemy tries to whisper in our ears in his efforts to get us to throw a pity party for ourselves and we are having trouble resisting the attack of the enemy, don't forget to use the leverage that belonging to the Lord Jesus gives.

We can even leverage His blood at the mercy seat. When we come before God and must give an account of our service and our use of what has been given to us, and we must lift imperfect hands before Him, but hands that did at least try to give their best, we can use the leverage of His blood and say, "I plead the blood."

BREAKING FINANCIAL BARRIERS

Eliminate Debt!

TEXT: II KINGS 4: 1-7

There is a simple formula for breaking financial barriers that consists of at least three steps: Honor God! Eliminate Debt. Build Assets! Our studies of the prophet Haggai showed us that those who do not honor God do not have God's favor. If we want God to bless and prosper us then we cannot neglect God. We must make God a priority. The prophet Malachi's teaching on the tithe is that if we do not give God the minimum 10% gross as our foundational expression of thanksgiving and praise, we remain under a curse. Solomon, history's wisest man has said, "Honor the Lord with your with your substance and with the first fruits of all your produce; then your barns will be filled with plenty, and your vats will be bursting with wine." After a discussion about such issues as food, shelter and clothing, the Lord Jesus instructed us, "Strive [Seek] first for the kingdom of God and his righteousness, and all these things will be given to you as well (Matthew 6: 33)." Our Lord has also promised, "give, and it will be given to you. A good measure, pressed down, shaken together, running over, will be put into your lap."

While honoring God with our tithes, offerings and money is a necessary first step towards breaking the financial barriers that block us from walking in the vision that God has for our lives, it is still only a first step. God will open up the windows of heaven and pour down an overflowing blessing and God will provide the increase, but not for us to waste and mess up. Honoring God with 10% will not overcome bad management of the 90% that we have left. Many of us have management issues that have created debt in our lives. We must honor God and we must also eliminate debt from our lives that is eating up the 90% and consuming part of the overflow. The reality is that many of us do not tithe and a number of us are not walking in the vision we know that God has for us is because of debt. We are so deep in debt we can't figure out how we are going to tithe and pay our bills. We are so deep in debt we cannot understand how we can possibly walk in the vision that God has shown us. If you ask some of us why we don't tithe or why we didn't start that business we have been talking about, or why didn't we go back to school like we have been talking about, or why we are not doing certain things that we have been wanting to do that will improve our situation, the first thing we will say is, "I can't afford it."

We are so deep in debt we are barely making it and we just can't see how we can afford to do anything more or anything other than what we are doing right now. The reality that a number of us who are followers of the Lord Jesus Christ face is how to get out of the deep financial holes we have dug for ourselves or that others have dug and continue to dig for us, or holes we fell into before we realized they were there. The issue I want us to wrestle with is what do we do about the debt that threatens to consume us even when we are honoring God first. The text is a case in point.

According to the word of God, a widow of one of Elisha's fellow prophets approached him because she had a debt problem. She said to the prophet Elisha, "Your servant my husband is dead; and you know that your servant feared the Lord, but a creditor has come to take my two children as slaves." The husband of this widow was a good God-fearing man. There is nothing in the record to indicate that he squandered his money or that he was wasteful with his resources in any way. From what little we know about him, however we know he made at least one major mistake. He did not secure his financial future and consequently he left his wife and children in financial jeopardy. Let me just say at the outset that no matter how spiritual we are, no matter how holy or anointed we are, no matter how faithful we are, no matter how much we love the Lord and how devoted to the church we may be, we still need to secure our financial future. Being spiritual does not exempt us from securing our financial future. Trusting in God to take care of us does not exempt us from doing our part to secure our financial future.

Counting on Social Security, Medicaid or Medicare or the government is not enough. Counting on the church or even the employers that we have worked for and given the best years of our life to, is not enough. The government, the church and some of our employers establish minimums, we ought to be looking at maximums. Sometimes we get so heaven bound and so intent on living in such a way that we can get to heaven, we fail to take care of some basic money matters on earth. The issue for our future is not only where we will spend eternity, but also planning ahead for our financial future while we are still here on earth. How will the last years of our life on earth be spent, in sufficiency or in scarcity, in prosperity or in poverty?

Somebody may ask, when do you start securing your financial future? Since today is the future of yesterday, and tomorrow is the future of today, we begin securing our financial future today. It is never too early to begin securing our financial future. And no matter how old we are, since we don't know how long we will be around, it is never too late to start securing our finances for whatever future we have left. After all Abraham did not become financially secure until he was in his eighties, and then he lived for another thirty-five years. In other words, if you are a child or a teenager and start receiving an allowance or get your first babysitting job or your first lawn mowing or snow shoveling or retail store job, put aside ten percent for the Lord and save ten percent for the future. If you are working, no matter how many bills you have, set aside something for your future. What you consistently set aside is not going to make or break you, but it can make a difference in the long run. And if you are retired, don't spend every penny of your Social Security and retirement check each month. Continue to set aside something so you will have something additional to draw on. When do we start securing our financial future? The time to start is now.

Now to return to the text: "Now the wife of a member of the company of the prophets cried to Elisha, 'Your servant my husband is dead; and you know that your servant feared the Lord, but a creditor has come to take my two children as slaves." Debt not only holds us in bondage and prevents us from walking in the vision God has for us, debt can reach out and grab others in our midst that are close to us and then it can reach forward and try to hold back and hold down those who come after us. A pile of debt handicaps those who come after us, while a foundation of financial security gives them a head start. We have an obligation to those who come after us just like we stand on the shoulders of those who came before us. Will we give those who come after us weak or strong financial shoulders to stand upon? Will we pass on good or bad financial examples to those who come after us? Will we pass on good or bad financial habits to those who come after us? Somebody needs to break the cycle of poverty, low aim, and mediocre living that has been in some of our families for generations and it might as well be us. Somebody needs to break the pattern of living beneath our privilege and not reaching our full financial potential. If not us who and if not now when?

This woman in the text swallowed her pride and went to Elisha and told him about her situation. Perhaps not with her, but with a number of us, pride is what puts and keeps us in poverty. We can't afford to run with a certain crowd and we can't afford to do and buy certain things and we are too proud to admit it. So we keep buying what we can't afford, we keep taking vacations and trips that we can't afford, we keep shopping in certain stores, and we keep living above our means so we can keep up false appearances. We keep digging ourselves deeper and deeper into a hole, because we are too proud to admit that we are in quicksand and we need help.

A few years ago I was in Brazil attending a conference and I had some free time so I decided to go shopping. I had a ministerial colleague whom I highly respected, who has since gone home to be with the Lord, and so I decided to ask her if she wanted to go with me. She told me, "Bill I would love to go, but shopping is my weakness so I can't go." As I thought about her answer I suspected she was in deep credit card debt and had put herself on a spending diet. I never suspected that this anointed woman of God who was a powerful preacher had such a problem with spending money that she could not go shopping. But my respect for her increased because she knew her weakness and was strong enough to say no, no matter what I thought. Don't let pride put you in and keep you in debt. Don't be afraid to admit you are having a problem and don't be afraid to seek help if you do. To begin with you are not the only one with financial issues. You would be surprised to learn how many together people you know, how many saved and accomplished people you know, that you have been feeling inferior to, have messed up financial situations. Then secondly the only way that you can clean up a mess, the only way you can solve a problem is by admitting that you have one.

When the woman came to Elisha, who was not a rich man, but who had access to the right resources because he was God's man, he asked her, "What shall I do for you? Tell me, what do you have in your house?" When you serve the Lord and you have financial issues never forget you have access to the right resources. There are always resources to solve your problems, the issue is whether are not you are going to use the right resources or the wrong resources. There are right resources and there are wrong resources. A resource that will solve an immediate problem but leave you in a worse position in the long run is the wrong resource. A resource that charges exorbitant interest so that you never get out of debt or whose life saving debt is a greater burden than the original drowning debt is the wrong resource. As the old preachers used to say, you don't dig a bigger hole in the backyard trying to fill up the one in the front yard. A resource that will require you to sell your soul, your integrity and your dignity is the wrong resource. A resource that will keep you under someone else's thumb or in slavery to someone else is the wrong resource. A resource that is in conflict with the word of God is the wrong resource. A resource that is not equally yoked with your spirit and your faith and your conscience is the wrong resource. A resource that you are ashamed to admit that you are using is the wrong resource. If you have to hide your resources from those who love you and have your best interests at heart that is the wrong resource. There are some resources the people of God should not be using to solve their problems. There are enough resources that God has for those who belong to him that they never have to play on the devils turf to survive. If you do not know the right resources, ask God in prayer to direct you to where you ought to go.

When the woman came to Elisha he asked her what she had in her house. That at first seems to be a strange question because if the woman had anything she would not have come to Elisha. However Elisha knew that God never leaves those who belong to him with nothing to work with. What we have to work with may not be much, but God has left us with something to work with. The prophet was correct because she replied, "Your servant has nothing in the house, *except* a jar of oil." Never underestimate the importance of whatever little you have to work with. Never underestimate the importance of your jar of oil. Never underestimate the importance of your *except.* Somebody said,

"I have nothing in the house except prayer. I have nothing in the house except faith. I have nothing in the house except a vision and a dream. I have nothing in the house except one friend or one person who believes in me. I have nothing in the house except determination. I have nothing in the house except a working mind and a committed heart. I have nothing in the house except a jar of oil."

Ask God to show you the jar of oil that you may be overlooking, which is the right resource for you to help you get out of debt. I repeat, do not underestimate the jars of oil and the "excepts" in your house. With nothing except a shepherd's rod God sent Moses to Egypt to free God's people from over 400 years of Egyptian bondage. With nothing except a march and a shout Joshua and the people of God brought down the walls of Jericho. With nothing except a slingshot David brought down Elijah. With nothing except a little oil in the cruse and a little meal, God kept his prophet Elijah and the widow of Zarephath and her son alive for three years while famine was in the land. With nothing except two fish and five barely loaves the Lord Jesus fed five thousand. And with nothing except an old rugged cross he redeemed our souls from a burning hell.

When the widow told Elisha about her jar of oil, he told her, "Go outside, borrow vessels from all your neighbors, empty vessels and not just a few. Then go in, and shut the door behind you and your children, and start pouring into all these vessels; when each is full, set is aside." In other words, Elisha gave her a plan to work with. Her debt problem was not immediately solved with the jar of oil. She had to have a plan that she had to work. Elimination of debt is not just a temporary fix, but is part of the way that we secure our financial future. To eliminate debt we must first admit that we have a problem and that we need help. We must then seek out the right resources. We must then look at what we have to work with. Then we need a plan that we must work. Either we plan our work or we plan to fail. Debt will not be eliminated because we pray. Debt will not be eliminated because we love the Lord and have a good heart and want to do the right thing. Debt will not be eliminated because we discover our jar of oil. We begin to eliminate debt when we match our jar of oil up with a plan and then work the plan. To eliminate debt we must plan our work and then work our plan.

Note, that the prophet told the woman to shut the door behind her. Why? Elisha knew that you do not need to let everybody know your business. You inform those who can help in some way or another but keep everybody else out of your financial business. Elisha knew that when you begin to make progress on getting out of debt and people sense that your situation may be surpassing theirs; jealousy and undercutting have a way of setting in. Some people will try to start taking their jars back. They will try to block the plan that looks like it will cause you to surpass them. Or those with a free loading spirit will come and try to take or borrow some of the oil you need to get on a firm footing. They will try to guilt you into letting them have your oil. When you are trying to get on your feet there will be those who will come to you and say, "What are you going to do with all of that oil? I have bills to pay to. I'm a little behind in my car note, my insurance, and my rent. I need a new pair of shoes or a dress. My car needs tires. My life is in danger riding on those bald tires. I need carfare for work. Shaneiqua needs to go the beauty parlor and Hassan needs some more sneakers. You ought to let me have some of that oil and quit being so cheap and stingy. You can afford it. After all we are neighbors. After all we are relatives. After all we belong to the same church. After all I knew you when you didn't have that oil." Before you can get your own oil situation straightened out here comes those with a freeloading spirit trying to get your blessing. Therefore shut the door and tell others to do what you did. Look for the jar in their own houses and come up with their own plans. If you start giving your oil out, they will keep coming back until you are out of oil. So shut the door and work your plan.

As the widow began to work her plan the oil kept flowing. As the widow did her part the oil supply multiplied. As a faithful follower of the Lord Jesus Christ when we do our part, and are faithful to the plan we have a right to expect miracles. We have a right to expect God to multiply our resources. We have a right to expect God to give us favor in unexpected places. We have a right to expect God to open doors that we had not seen and did not know were there. We have a right to expect God to make ways out of no ways. We have a right to expect God to rebuke the devourer. We have a right to expect God to be God in our situation and do what only God can do. When we do our part and are faithful to the plan expect oil to keep on flowing.

The widow's boy kept bringing jars and the woman kept pouring and the oil kept flowing. The oil kept flowing until the boy came into the house and said, "There are no more vessels." Then the oil stopped. The oil did not stop flowing until the boy said that they had no more capacity to hold what God was pouring into their lives. God's favor does not stop until there is some lack on our part. It may be a lack of obedience or a lack of faith or a satisfied spirit that loses some of its hunger or thirst or drive to get to the next level. But God never stops blessing until there is some lack on our part. When it comes to blessing his children, when it comes to blessing those who seek God's face and delight themselves in God's presence, when it comes to blessing those who love God for who God is, God does not know the meaning of the word enough. When it comes to those who are faithful to following God's vision, God does not know the meaning of the word enough. That is why when Jesus was raised after he was faithful to the plan for our redemption and was obedient even to death on the cross; he was raised with all power in heaven and earth in his hands. That is why he has a name higher than any name that at the name Jesus every knee shall bow and every tongue shall confess that Jesus Christ is Lord to the glory of God the Father. That is why he reigns forever. When we are faithful God does not know the meaning of the word enough. God keeps on blessing. "What no eye has seen, nor ear heard, nor the human heart conceived, what God has prepared for those who love him. (I Corinthians 2: 9)" "Beloved, we are God's children now; what we will be has not yet been revealed. What we do know is this: when he is revealed, we will be like him, for we will see him as he is (I John 3: 2)."

Never forget that God's desire and willingness to bless is always beyond our capacity and capability to receive. That is why we should never be hesitant to ask God for what we need, because God's ability to bless is always beyond our capacity to receive. When God says yes, his ability to bless us with what we have asked for is always beyond our capacity to hold it all. And when God says no to our prayers God's ability to sustain and bless in other ways is always beyond our ability and expectations to receive. That is why we have eternal life, because God's ability to bless is beyond the capacity of this life on earth to hold it all. Therefore God has designed eternity so that we can keep on enjoying forever and ever, God's ability to bless.

In the text, when the oil stopped flowing, the woman went to the prophet Elisha to tell him about all that had happened. He told her to sell the oil, pay the creditors and live off of the rest. In other words after she had paid her debt she had something to live on. She had some leftover blessings. When the widow came to Elisha she wanted just enough help to solve her immediate problem. She wanted just enough to pay her bills and prevent the creditor from taking her children. However when God got through taking care of her situation, she not only had her immediate problem solved, she had something left over to live on. After she had paid her bills she had enough money left over from the sale of her oil to keep on living.

Any number of believers can testify to the leftover blessings of God? When Moses stayed in the presence of God on Mount Sinai, there was so much glory on him that when he left the presence of God, the leftover glory leftover on his face continued to glow and he had to wear a veil. For days he was able to bask in the leftover glory that came from being in the presence of God. When the disciples distributed the lunch of two fish and five barley loaves, the Lord Jesus told them to go back through the crowd and gather up the fragments so that nothing would be left. The disciples gathered twelve baskets full of leftovers that gave them something to live on. When the Day of Pentecost came on the early church holy wind blew through the house where they were gathered and holy fire fell upon each worshipper. There was such a manifest presence of God, there was such an anointing leftover on Peter that he preached with such power that three thousand souls joined the church that day. When the experience was over the believers had enough anointing left over that they continued to live in love and harmony; signs and wonders continued to be done among them and the Lord added daily souls who were being saved.

When God helps you get out of debt, God will give you enough oil so that you will have something left over to keep on living. When the Lord brings you out of that situation you will have a testimony about the goodness of God. That testimony will be your leftover blessing that will help you to keep on living. Consequently if you ever get into trouble again, and if you get your back up against the wall again, and you begin to wonder if you can make it. Think about the testimony that you have about how God saved you last time, and that leftover testimony will encourage you to keep on living, to keep on pressing your way, to keep on praying until the breakthrough comes in your latest crisis.

No true worship service is simply about the inspiration of the moment, it is about having leftover power when the service is ended so that when you meet the devil after church, there will be enough word leftover to keep you grounded. When you meet him in your home there will be enough anointing leftover so that your spirit will not be broken. When you meet the devil on the job or school, there will be enough power for you to hold your head up and keep your eye on the goal. When you meet the discouragement among your friends, co-workers, and various family and church members during the week, there will be enough conviction left over for you to keep on living.

We serve a Savior that was crucified on Calvary some two thousand years ago. When He died, His blood was shed to cleanse the world from sin. However even though He died a long time ago, the Gospel that we proclaim, believe and know to be true is this— -there is still enough love leftover for you and me even now. There is still enough forgiveness leftover to give you and me another chance even now. There is still enough cleansing and deliverance leftover that is available for you and me even now.

BREAKING FINANCIAL BARRIERS

Build Your Assets!

TEXT: GENESIS 13: 2

According to the text, Abraham, the father of the faithful, was not only the first tither listed in the Bible, he is also the first person in scripture who is described as being rich. I do not want to give the impression that when we tithe we will automatically become rich. However, when we look at the fact that Abraham who was the first tither was also the first person in the scriptures mentioned as being rich, that fact is confirmation of the truth from the prophet Malachi. That those who tithe receive such an overflow they barely have room enough to receive it. Later in this chapter tension arises between Abraham and his nephew Lot, who received some of the overflow from Abraham's abundance because the place where they were was not adequate...there was not room enough, the grazing land and watering holes were insufficient to take care of all of their livestock.

Sometimes the overflow will come in the form of money and sometimes the overflow will come in the form of miracles. Sometimes the overflow will come in the form of riches and sometimes it will come in the form of revelation. Sometimes the overflow will come in the form of finances and sometimes it will come in the form of friends and family. Sometimes the overflow will come in the form of livestock and sometimes it will come in the form of life and love. Sometimes the overflow will come in the form of silver and sometimes it will come in the form of strength. Sometimes the overflow will come in the form of gold and sometimes it will come in the form of grace. Abraham, the father of the faithful who was the first tither in the Bible, and who was also the first person listed in the scriptures as rich, demonstrates that when we give in faith, and honor the Lord with our substance, we will receive some kind of overflow.

What is interesting to me is that when God came to Abraham and told him to leave the place where he was and journey to a place God would show him, God did not say that Abraham would end up rich. God told Abraham God would make of him a great nation, God would make his name great, and God would so bless Abraham that through him all of the families of the earth would be blessed. That was the word God spoke to Abraham at the beginning of chapter 12. However, at the beginning of chapter 13 we are told that Abraham was rich in livestock, in gold and in silver. How did Abraham get so rich between chapter 12 and chapter 13? We do not know, exactly. All we know is that as Abraham was obedient to the vision God had for his life and obedient to the word of instruction from God, God prospered him. As Abraham did what God told him to do, God supplemented, added to and blessed Abraham in ways Abraham did not expect.

The promises God makes to us are awesome enough. The promises of God are sufficient enough to cover any sacrifice we must make, or think we are making, to be faithful and obedient. The promises of God are rewarding enough. The promises of God are miraculous enough to make them appear unbelievable when we use the litmus tests of logic and human understanding and possibility. However, the blessings God gives us beyond what is promised when we are faithful to the vision, and when we are obedient to the word and will of God, leave us mystified, humbled and grateful beyond words.

Consequently, every time praise goes forth among saints, there are always at least four categories of praise. There are those who give God praise simply because God is worthy. There are those who give God praise because of the promises God has already kept. There are those who give God praise in advance for promises made to them that God is going to keep. Then, there are those who give God praise for the unexpected supplement God added to a word and revelation that was already rich beyond expectations. The fact that Abraham was so blessed beyond what was promised demonstrated the truth again that we cannot beat God giving and that God will be indebted to none of us.

We do not know exactly how Abraham became rich as he followed the word and the vision of God for his life. All we know is that as Abraham followed the vision God had for his life God helped him amass or gather assets. To break financial barriers that block us from seeing, receiving or following God's vision for our lives we must do at least three simple things. We must honor God. We must eliminate debt. And, we must build assets. We must honor God because the vision comes from God as does the health and strength needed to pursue vision. We also need God to protect and help us manage whatever God brings into our lives.

Then we must eliminate debt because our consumer debt is bondage pure and simple. Debt is the enemy of financial freedom. Debt blocks our breakthroughs to an anxiety free life. Debt is a weight that works against our net worth. Debt is a burden that belittles our blessings. Debt is a flood that drowns dreams and it is a fire that consumes freedom. Debt is a rifle that shoots us down. Debt is quicksand that pulls us down and debt is a stronghold that keeps us down. We will never be able to fully pursue the vision God has for our lives when we are saddled down with debt that keeps us going around in circles just to keep up. A number of us know what it is to get our cars stuck in the mud or the snow. We press the gas and our tires spin but we go nowhere. We work hard and we work long, but we go nowhere because our debt keeps us stuck in the same place year after year. We have motion but no forward movement. As long as we are in debt to somebody or some institution, others have the last word not we even though our name may be listed as owner.

Then, we must build assets. In life we have either assets or liabilities. An asset is a resource that adds value to our lives. A liability is a drawback or a disadvantage. How do we determine if something or someone is an asset to our lives? We look at whether or not they add value. How do we feel after the experience or how do we feel after we have been with them or talked with them? Has the experience, whether it is at church or a conversation, added anything of value to our lives? If we feel affirmation then it or they are assets, but if we feel anxiety then it or they are liabilities. If we feel better then it or they are assets, but if we feel burdened then it or they are liabilities. If we feel caring then it or they are assets, but if we feel coldness, then it or they are liabilities. If we feel defended then it or they are assets, but if we feel defeated then it or they are liabilities. If we feel delivered then it or they are assets, but if we feel demeaned then it or they are liabilities. If we feel delight then it or they are assets, but if we feel dread then it or they are liabilities. If we feel enlightened then it or they are assets, but if we feel empty then it or they are liabilities. If we feel faith or faithfulness then it or they are assets, but if we feel fickleness then it or they are liabilities.

If we feel fulfilled then it or they are assets, but if we feel like a fool then it or they are liabilities. If we feel as if we are growing then it or they are assets, but if we feel like groaning then it or they are liabilities. If we feel good then it or they are assets, but if we feel guilty then it or they are liabilities. If we feel hopeful then it or they are assets, but if we feel hopeless, then it or they are liabilities. If we feel helped then it or they are assets, but if we feel hindered then it or they are liabilities. If we feel healing then it or they are assets, but if we feel hurt then it or they are liabilities. If we feel loved then it or they are assets, but if we feel lonely then it or they are liabilities. If we feel power then it or they are assets, but if we feel put down then it or they are liabilities. If we feel rewarded then it or they are assets, but if we feel revulsion then it or they are liabilities. If we feel stronger then it or they are assets, but if we feel stifled then it or they are liabilities. If we feel useful then it or they are assets, but if we feel used then it or they are liabilities. If we feel understanding then it or they are assets, but if we feel undervalued then it or they are liabilities. If we feel worth then it or they are assets, but if we feel worthless then it or they are liabilities.

Let us never forget that vision is about adding value to our lives. Therefore if we are to pursue God's vision for our lives we must work on increasing our assets and doing something about our liabilities. We need to work on changing a liability into an asset or else we remove the liability, but we should not just allow a liability to remain a liability forever. When Joseph told his brothers what they meant for evil God used it for good, he was able to change his liability of being sold into slavery into an asset for saving others. When the Lord Jesus transformed persecuting Saul on the Damascus Road into preaching Paul, he changed a liability into an asset. When the

Lord Jesus transformed an old rugged cross from an emblem of shame into a symbol of salvation, he turned a liability into an asset. It is possible to turn liabilities into assets. When people do mean things to us and try to stop us and we become that much more determined to succeed, that is turning liabilities into assets. When the devil trips us up or we make mistakes and instead of staying down we learn our lessons and get back up, wipe ourselves off and keep going with the wisdom that we received from our fall, that is turning our liabilities into assets. When the Lord helps us to turn enemies into friends, and detractors into supporters, and rumors into our marketing and public relations campaigns, that is turning liabilities into assets.

We can work on changing a liability into an asset or we can remove the liability. In this thirteenth chapter Abraham removed one of his liabilities. When Abraham received the call to leave where he was and go to a new place for his life he took his nephew Lot along with him. As Abraham prospered so did Lot. Everything Lot had he received because of his association with Abraham. Lot added little to Abraham's life, but he received the spillover from Abraham's obedience and faith journey. However in this chapter when the place where they settled turned out to be insufficient to hold both of their flocks and herds, rather than Lot coming up with a suggestion, Abraham came up with one. He suggested that they separate and go their respective ways. Since Abraham could not turn his nephew into an asset, he suggested that they separate. Abraham gave Lot the choice of the land that was before him. Lot as the younger of the two, as the one who had been blessed through his uncle's obedience to the vision and word from God, should have chosen the less desirable portion of the land. Yet Lot chose the best part for himself and left the less desirable part to this uncle to whom he owed everything. After Lot left Abraham God appeared to Abraham and told him not to worry about the better portion that Lot chose, because everything as far as his eye could see, would be his.

When Abraham put some distance between he and his liability, God told him that even though he had already been blessed beyond his expectations, what he had was just the beginning of what God would give him. Even though we are blessed and highly favored, we can only receive so much when we carry certain liabilities with us. Consequently, if we cannot change our liabilities into assets, then like Abraham we should consider putting some distance between them and us. If they or it are not adding anything to your life perhaps you ought to think about subtracting them. Put some conversational distance between you and them. Put some mental distance between you and them. Put some prayer distance between you and them. Put some spatial distance between you and them. Quit sharing your heart with them since all they are going to do is look out for themselves or discourage you from pursuing the vision God has for you since they feel threatened by your growth. Quit spending so much time with them. If all they are doing is draining you and putting you down, don't feel guilty about making a decision not hang out or spend so much time doing something or being with someone who is a weight on your spirit and a hole in your pocketbook. If you have a liability and you do not know what to do about it or him or her or them, ask the Lord to show you what to do about them because your own ability to get and keep assets will be affected when you have to baby sit and care for so many liabilities.

"Now Abraham was very rich, in livestock and silver and gold." As Abraham pursued the vision God had for him, he also built up his assets. The key to breaking the back of the financial barriers that block vision is the strengthening of our asset base. I would submit to you that we need at least three major assets. We already have two to start with, and if we use the two we already have correctly, we can get the third. The first major asset we all have is God. Since God gives the vision, God will also provide the provision. When we have God on our side who owns the cattle on a thousand hills, the thousand hills, and the water underneath the thousand hills that grows the grass that feeds the cattle, we are already on the road to prosperity. When we have God on our side, who knows everything about everything and everyone, we already have an unfailing source who can direct us to a proper investment. I read a lot of investment books and people give all kinds of investment advice. However, very few people suggest asking God to direct us about how we are to build our asset base. Yet the word of God plainly instructs us, "Trust in the Lord with all your heart and do not lean on your own understanding, in all your ways acknowledge [God] and God will direct your path. " (Proverbs 3: 5-6) Jesus told us plainly, "Ask and it would be given you; search and you will find; knock and the door will be opened to you. (Matthew 7: 7)" James tells us, "If any of you is lacking in wisdom; ask God, who gives to all generously and ungrudgingly, and it will be given to you. (James 1: 5)" Do your homework and your research, listen to the experts, but don't forget to ask God for direction and guidance. When we have God who is still able to work miracles and do the impossible, we are already on the road to recovery from our mistakes and our poverty. Remember, God wants us to do well more than we do. Jesus told us that it was our Father's pleasure to give us the kingdom.

As I have said before, God who gave the vision is more invested in our success and well-being than we are. God, who has numbered the very hairs on our heads and has come in the flesh with a face and personality known as Jesus Christ, is more invested in our success than we are. Why be jealous of anybody when you have God on your side? Why do you feel that life has dealt you a bad hand when you have God on your side? When you have God on your side, you have who you need to turn losing hands into winning hands. When you have God on your side, why are you taking abuses from other people and why are you allowing others to hold you in bondage and your gifts and talents in captivity? When you have God on your side why are you so fearful that unless you have certain people in your life you can't make it? When you have God on your side why are you allowing other folk, with their limited perspective and power, talk you out of the vision God has shown you? When you have God on your side, why are you still sitting around feeling guilty and whining about mistakes you have made? When you have God on your side why are you talking about how old or how young you are, or who does not like you or who is against you? When you have God on your side, why are you talking about how difficult or impossible the task is? When you have God on your side why are you talking about what you can't do? To break the financial barriers in our lives we need to understand that we already have the greatest asset we need and that asset is the eternal God who is our refuge and strength, and our very present help in a time of trouble who was incarnated in Jesus Christ and who as the Holy Spirit abides with us and in us to empower us for the living of these days.

Our first and greatest asset is God, in all of God's fullness, Father, Son and Holy Spirit. Our next greatest asset is ourselves. That's right, your next greatest asset is you. When we think about assets, most of us first think of others. We always like to think of who we know and whom we can get to help us. Well the first person you know is you and you are the person you have to begin working with and strengthening and building up. If you don't believe in you, nobody else will. If you are going to get anywhere in life you first have to sell yourself and the first customer or client you have to sell yourself to is you. People who don't think much of themselves do not end up with much because they have "dissed," written off, rejected and discounted one of the best things they have going for them. People who look in a mirror and cannot appreciate what they see do not end up with very much because no one is going to invest in anyone who does not exhibit self-confidence and self-respect. People who are always putting themselves down do not end up with very much because they focus on what they lack and not what they have. People who always walk around saying, "I ain't nothing" or "Ain't much to me," end up with nothing because nothing draws and attracts nothing. People who don't think much of themselves have insulted God because you are the creation of God and God does not create inferior or second-rate merchandise. Who do you think you are to insult God by putting down part of God's creation, which you represent? You are what you have to work with, so quit complaining about what you don't have. Team up with your number one resource who is God because great, marvelous and miraculous things can happen when you and God get together.

Never underestimate what we can do, how far we can go and how high we can rise when God and we get together. Noah had a tendency to get drunk but when he and God got together, he became the father of a new generation after the flood. Abraham and Sarah were too old to have children but when they and God got together, they became patriarchs of the faith long after childbearing days were done. Moses was a murderer and a stutterer, but when he and God got together, he became God's spokesperson and liberator for an enslaved people. David had a zipper problem but when he and God got together he became Israel's greatest king and the man after God's own heart. Mary of Nazareth was an ordinary handmaiden, but when she and the Holy Spirit got together, she brought forth God's only begotten Son. Simon Peter was a foul-mouthed fisherman, but when he and Jesus got together he became a preacher of power. Saul of Tarsus was a persecutor of the church but when he and Jesus got together he became the faith's greatest missionary. If God did it for them, never underestimate what God will bring into and out of your life when you as asset number two team up with God who is asset number one.

Because Abraham teamed up with God he was able to acquire the third kind of assets, which are appreciating assets. In Abraham's culture, livestock, silver and gold were considered to be appreciating assets. There are two kinds of assets—depreciating and appreciating assets. Depreciating assets lose their value in time, but appreciating assets gain value in time. Most us of invest in depreciating assets such as cars, clothes, appliances, vacations, and things that are good to have but which loses value over time. We need to focus more on appreciating assets such as real estate, home ownership, businesses to match our personality, skill sets and training, further education and self improvement, health care, the education of our children and grandchildren, and money that is saved and invested in the instruments that the Lord has directed us to. Depreciating assets are good for today, but appreciating assets are looking towards tomorrow. Depreciating assets are good for the moment but appreciating assets are about the momentous. Depreciating assets will provide a smile for the present, but appreciating assets are about security for the future. Depreciating assets decrease in time, but appreciating assets increase and lengthen into eternity.

No matter how much we pay for cars, no matter what brand they are, no matter what options they have on them, the minute we drive them off the lot, they lose some of their value. To break the financial barriers that block vision we need to devote ourselves to that which not only holds value but also adds value. That is why I enjoy inviting people to meet Jesus because He holds His value. It has been two thousand years since He walked among us and preached and taught, but his truth still holds value. His truth and his promises and his word are as reliable now as they were when He spoke them. His truth still stands; He still keeps promises; and we can still stake our lives upon his word. It has been two thousand years since He fed five thousand with two fish and five barley loaves, and his provision still holds value. He is still able to supply our needs according to his riches in glory. It has been two thousand years since he walked on water and calmed the raging sea, but his power over storms and his power in storms still hold its value. Even now He will keep us from drowning and from destruction although we are going through the greatest storm in our lives.

It has been two thousand years since He gave his life on Calvary and his blood still holds its value. It will still cleanse the foulest sin. It has been two thousand years since He prayed from a cross, "Father forgive them for they know not what they do (Luke 23: 34)," but his forgiveness still holds value. For, "if we confess our sins, He who is faithful and just will forgive our sins and cleanse us from all unrighteousness (I John 1: 9)." It has been two thousand years since He told a dying thief, "Today you shall be with me in Paradise (Luke 23: 43)." Yet his salvation and his deliverance still hold value. No matter who we are and no matter what we have done, He still saves to the utmost. It has been two thousand years since He rose from the grave but his resurrection still holds value. "We know that when this earthly tent of this tabernacle is dissolved we have another building, a house not made with hands, eternal in the heavens (II Corinthians 5: 1)."

Not only does He hold value but He also appreciates in value. The longer you live with Him, and the more you have to live through with Him, the more valuable He becomes. You think that He is valuable in the sunshine, walk with Him in the rain and the more valuable He becomes. You think that He is valuable in good times, walk with Him in bad times and the more valuable He becomes. You think that He is valuable when you are up, let Him walk with you when you are down, and the more valuable He will become. You think that He is valuable when you have money, walk with Him, trust Him, lean upon Him, when you do not know how you are going to make it and the more valuable He becomes. You think He is valuable when you have a job, lose your job and the more valuable He becomes. You think He is valuable when you are healthy, walk with Him in sickness, and the more valuable He becomes. You think He is valuable, when you have; but walk with Him when you have experienced a loss and the more valuable He becomes.

However what I like most about Him is not only does He continue to appreciate in value, but He also appreciates the value of those who turn their lives over to Him. I once saw a sale sign on some shirts that said, "Slightly soiled; greatly reduced in value." Have you been losing value lately? You started off with so much potential, so many good intentions, so many dreams and so many hopes. But since you have been traveling through life you have begun to feel as if you are losing value and are becoming a depreciating asset. Has life made you a deprecating asset? Has sin soiled you and reduced your value and made you feel like a depreciating asset in your eyes as well as the eyes of others? Has your past and your mistakes; that unwanted pregnancy, that fall from innocence, that failure to keep your vows, that season of addiction and bondage, made you feel like a depreciating asset in your eyes and in the eyes of others? Has divorce and heartbreak, that rape, abuse and misuse made you feel like a depreciating asset and reduced your value in your own eyes as well as the eyes of others? Has that setback in your career and that public embarrassment made you feel as if you have lost value and have become a depreciating asset? Has age or sickness, and the fact that you can't do what you once did, reduced your value in your own eyes and made you feel like a depreciating asset? I know somebody who will increase your value and turn you from a depreciating into an appreciating asset. Paul said, "If any one is in Christ he or she is a new creation; old things are passed away, behold all things have become new (II Corinthians 5: 17)."

BREAKING FINANCIAL BARRIERS

Our Real Net Worth

TEXT: LUKE 12: 13-21 (emphasis 13-15)

Some time ago I went to the doctor for my annual check up. Part of that check up involved me stepping on a scale so that he could get an accurate reading of my weight. I had not disrobed at that point and asked him if he wanted me to do so. He replied no and so I got up on the scale with my clothes on. When I saw my weight I was surprised because it was more than I had been estimating and more than my ego had supposed it to be. Even though there is a scale in my bathroom, I am not one of these persons who weighs himself every day, because I do not want to start off every day depressed. I asked the doctor, "Are you sure you don't want me to take off some of these clothes?" He was not as concerned about what the scale was showing as I was, so he said, "No, Reverend that's not necessary." I said, "I know, but out of curiosity let me just take off a couple of items and then let's see what the scale says." As he patiently looked at me, 1 then proceeded to take off my shoes and my pants and got back on the scale. The items I took off made a slight difference in what the scale recorded as my weight, very slight. However I still weighed more than I had been pretending.

As I thought about this incident I was reminded that when it comes to weight a number of us deal with three figures. First, there is the weight that we imagine or claim we are until reality or the truth of the scale sets in. Secondly, there is the weight we have with our clothes on. Then, third there is what I call our real net weight, which is what we weigh with our clothes off. One of the underlying principles of our approach to breaking the financial barriers that block vision is that God has a vision of our lives that is greater than any vision that we can have for ourselves or that others can have for us. However we recognize that many of us are not prepared to claim that vision, believe that vision or walk into that vision. Due to so many financial issues like strangling and encumbering debt, we can't see how it is possible at our age and stage in life to reach what God has shown us or where we would like to be. Our problem is not that we do not have faith or that we are not filled with the Holy Spirit or that we do not pray or read the word of God or worship on a regular basis. Our problem is not our failure to tithe. We are good, saved, responsible, and honorable Christian people. We can do all of these things but if we do not manage the other ninety percent well, after giving God the ten percent, we can and will still have financial barriers that block us from walking in the vision God has for us.

A number of us do not have a sufficiency problem, a number of us have a management problem. We have sufficient to take care of our basic necessities. However, because we do not manage well what we have, we have become encumbered with so much debt, we are having trouble taking care of our necessities, which makes us think that our problem is a lack and that we need more. The reality is, if we had the more we constantly are trying to get, and are continually asking God for, we would mismanage or mess that up as well. If we cannot manage little, we will not be able to manage much. Consequently many of us find ourselves in financial quicksand; the more we struggle with debt and other financial issues the deeper we sink. We have asserted that God does not desire us to live in financial bondage and no matter what the culture asserts, debt is not necessary and debt does not have to be the norm for our lives. We have further asserted that if we honor God with our lives and money, eliminate debt and build appreciating assets we can reach financial freedom and even financial prosperity. The issue I want to wrestle with in this message is how do we determine our real net worth. In other words, is our net worth based upon our having a certain dollar amount in the bank? And, if we do not have a particular dollar amount, does that mean we are a failure?

As we address this issue 1 would propose that we tend to determine our net worth in the same way we look upon our weight. Many of us base our understanding of our worth based on a financial figure or an ideal or vision or goal we would like to reach, that is somewhere between well off and very rich. We say things like, if we could just have two to three million dollars or even one, or ten million, or a hundred million and some of us even fantasize about being billionaires, then we would be all right. Some of us would be content with just enough to live comfortably. The problem is that a number of us have never defined what comfortable is. What is comfortable for us? Is comfortable enough for us to pay our bills every month without stressing? Does comfortable enough mean that we have enough to travel whenever we would like to, whether we do so or not?

Does comfortable mean we have enough to meet whatever unexpected medical or health expenses that may arise, or other kinds of crises or emergencies without being financially wiped out? Does comfortable mean we will have enough to live on, no matter what happens with inflation or with the economy? Does comfortable mean owning your own home or additional houses? Does comfortable mean affording some luxuries like a boat? Does comfortable mean we will have enough to live on without stressing, be able to give to some of our favorite charities and other causes and then leave something behind for some of our favorite loved ones, as well as those charities and causes? Or does comfortable mean the next level beyond where we are presently? What are our benchmarks for being comfortable and what does comfortable really mean to us? How do we know when we have gotten there? I would submit to you, if we have never really defined comfortable, then we will always live with a measure of discomfort or even fear of not having enough.

As we think about what financial comfort or financial security is for us, we must also recognize the fact that many of us have our definitions of what it means to be financially well off or comfortable or prosperous, determined by the culture we operate in or by others. Many of us go into debt because society or others tell us that to be a success means we ought to have this or that, or so much of this or that. Or, our egos tell us that to prove to our friends and family that we have arrived we need certain things. I remember when I first decided to buy the truck, after talking about it for several years. I knew

I could get a good deal on a Chevy, so I told my son and son in law of my plans. They told me, "Dad you don't want to get a Chevy because at this point in your life and with your status you should get a Lexus or a Mercedes." I told them that I already had a Mercedes and my ego did not need another one, and I knew what I wanted to pay and that was what I was going to pay. They then told me about some other trucks or SUV's that I should look at which were beyond my budget. I told them I was not interested. We had a couple of hours, so they took me to a Cadillac dealership. They figured that since I was interested in a GM product they would start with the Cadillac. I told them I was not interested in purchasing a Cadillac truck and so we left there and went to a Lincoln Mercury dealer. I told them again that I was not trying to buy luxury, status, or ego and to take me to a Chevrolet dealership. They eventually did and by the time I got through adding in all of the options I probably could have bought one of the other brands. But I bought what I wanted. Many times we allow the culture or others to dictate what our worth is based on and standards others set for us. Consequently we go into debt trying to live up to the worth that is defined for us by others.

Some of us determine our worth based upon definitions others impose upon us and some of us determine our worth based upon standards we impose upon ourselves. We determine we need to have certain stuff to prove to ourselves that we have made it and that we are a success. We use the standard of what our Lord calls "the abundance of possessions." to determine worth. As clothes add ounces and pounds to our weight, so our stuff adds weight to our worth. However I would submit that our real net worth, like our real weight, is determined by how we view ourselves without our stuff and without the extra pounds that our possessions, our associations and affiliations, and our title add to us. Many of us don't pursue the vision God has for us because we have such low self-esteem. What God has shown us is so good, it just seems impossible and beyond us to reach—someone else maybe, but not us. Why do some of us have such low self-esteem? Some of our self-esteem issues have to do with our backgrounds and things that have happened in the past. Some of our low self-esteem issues are due to mistakes and failures we have made in the past. But some of us have self-esteem issues because we do not have the kind of stuff or possessions that add the extra pounds or weight we need to help us feel good about ourselves. That is why we keep buying more possessions. We need the stuff to add weight to our worth. We need to hear again the words of the Lord, "a person's life does not consist in the abundance of possessions."

According to the text, someone approached the Lord Jesus with the request, " 'Teacher, tell my brother to divide the family inheritance with me.' The Lord told him, 'Friend, who set me to be a judge or arbitrator over you...Take care! Be on your guard against all kinds of greed: for one's life does not consist in the abundance of possessions." The person's request that the Lord ask his brother to divide the family inheritance with him sounds reasonable. However the Lord told him to be on guard against greed. Perhaps the Lord sensed another spirit in the person making the request besides desiring a share in the family inheritance. The issue is not simply possessions or prosperity but the spirit that is motivating us. There is nothing wrong in desiring more and in wanting nice things. However we need to watch the spirit that is motivating us. Nice things and the desire for more should never be used to add weight to our self worth. We need to understand we have worth that is beyond what we own. We are not to be defined by our possessions but by our purpose. Our character not our clothes define our worth. Our commitments and our convictions, not our careers define our worth. Our anointing not our automobiles defines our worth. Our hope not our houses define our worth. Our love not land defines our worth. Out testimony, not things define our worth. Our faith and our faithfulness, not our fashions determine our worth. Our relationship, not our material riches determine our worth. Our God not our goods determine worth.

To get our real weight, we have to strip down and take off of what hides the bulges and the wrinkles. Wholesome self-worth means that we can love and appreciate ourselves and feel good about ourselves even if we do not have all of the trappings and all of the other stuff to hide behind. When we take our clothes off we not only get our true weight we see ourselves as we really are, without our foundation garments and the colors and the clothes that we wear to hide our bulges, our cellulite, our stretch marks, and some of our blemishes and wrinkles. Perhaps the reason that some of us try to attain so much stuff, even if we have to go into debt to do it, and even if we can't really afford it, is that we are trying to hide some bulges and blemishes, some wrinkles and some stretch marks in our confidence, our self-esteem, in our relationships, and in our personalities. We are afraid that if the people saw the real us without all of the trappings that are around us, they would not really love us. As a matter of fact, sometimes we don't like the way we look either.

I want us as the children of God to prosper financially and be in good health. I want us to overcome and break every financial and other barrier that is blocking us from walking in the vision God has for us. I pray that we will get everything God has for us spiritually, financially, educationally, and in our relationships. However whether or not we prosper materially and financially, we need to understand we have worth and value beyond the "abundance of possessions." It is the worth beyond possessions that God sees and values. That is one of the lessons that comes to us from the parable the Lord told. He said, "The land of a rich man produced abundantly. And he thought to himself, 'What should I do, for I have no place to store my crops? Then he said,' I will do this: I will pull down my barns and build larger ones, and then I will store all my grain and my goods. I will say to my soul, Soul, you have ample goods laid up for many years; relax, eat, drink, be merry.' But God said to him, 'You fool! This very night your life is being demanded of you. And the things you have prepared, whose will they be?' So it is with those who store up treasures for themselves but are not rich towards God."

The man a number of us would have called a success God called a fool. God has a different standard for measuring worth. Aren't you glad God has a different standard for measuring worth? The only reason some of us are alive, the only reason some of us are where we are, the only reason some of us were spared or that some of us escaped that situation the enemy had planned to take us out, is that God has a different standard for measuring worth. The only reason that explains why some of us are preachers and others of us are leaders and members of the church is that God has a different standard for measuring worth. The world looked at our mistakes and missteps, the world looked at our mess-ups and our miscalculations and said we did not deserve another chance. The world looked at our color or our gender or our sexual preference and our family tree and our financial balance sheet and said we would never amount to much and that nothing much should be expected from us. The world looked at our addictions and our afflictions, our weaknesses and our wanderings and said we were a disgrace and should be damned. But God looked beyond our faults and not only saw our needs, but saw some worth in us that others did not care enough to see or try to find.

When I went to college my father was the pastor of a church that paid him $65.00 a week. However even with that salary I was in better shape than a number of children in my neighborhood. I had two parents at home. My father was considered a professional, even if he was only making $65.00 a week. Thus when I went to college, like most of those in my neighborhood, I needed financial aid. In my neighborhood when you talked about going to college you also talked in the same breath about scholarships and financial aid. Thus when I went to college it did not occur to me that there might have been students at college who were not filling out financial aid forms like I was. I began to notice something different when I drove my high school graduation gift to school, a 1948 Mercury, and parked it on the lot next to all of the shiny late model 1960 cars that many of my fellow students were driving. In my neighborhood, there were a number of old cars and so my car fit right in. However on that campus, my car stood out because it was the oldest one on the lot.

Then, when I filled out the financial aid form and listed our household income and looked up what the poverty line was, I discovered my father's income was ranked below the poverty line, and that I was considered to be living in poverty. That was when I discovered how poor my family was. I will always be grateful for growing up in a Christian home with Christian parents who used different standards from the world to determine self-worth; a home that taught me I was as good as anybody else and that I could go as far as I desired with God on my side, Christ in my heart, and the power of the Holy Spirit upon me. I would urge parents and grandparents that we have to use a different standard to teach self-worth besides designer clothes and name brand appliances and cars. Whereas the world measures self-worth by the size of the wallet or pocketbook, we serve a God who puts a tape measure around our hearts, our dreams and our faith.

The rich man in the parable had a lot of possessions to add weight to his worth but God saw that underneath all of the trappings, he had a very selfish, self centered and self-glorifying spirit. He did not even consider giving anything to any of the poor people that were around him. He did not even think about blessing or mentoring any young people so he might be able to pass on his knowledge to another generation. He did not even think about helping anybody out who was trying to get started in business or in their profession, who needed somebody to believe in them and help provide some resources to them. He did not even think about giving God any glory or contributing to the temple with his excess. The words of the Psalmist did not cross his mind when he said, "What shall I render to the Lord for all his bounty to me? I will lift up the cup of salvation and call on the name of the Lord, I will pay my vows to the Lord in the presence of all his people (Psalm 116: 12-14)." The words of Proverbs never even crossed his mind, "Honor the Lord with your substance and with the first fruits of all your produce; then your barns will be filled with plenty, and your vats will be bursting with wine (Proverbs 3: 9-10)." All the man in the parable could think about was his pleasure and his well-being. Consequently when the Lord looked at him he saw very little apart from his possessions. He saw shallowness and selfishness instead of substance. Thus God called him a fool and pronounced judgment upon him.

God determines our real worth. When I read the Gospels and they tell me that God so loved each and every one of us that he gave his only Son so that whoever believes in that Son should not perish but have everlasting life, then we must have worth far beyond what we own. How much are we worth? We have worth that is priceless. We have worth that can only be measured by the blood of God's own Son, even Jesus Christ our Lord. We have worth that is so great that God has taken the time to number the very hairs on our heads. We have worth that is so great that God created us in his very own image. We have worth that is so great that God makes and keeps every promise God makes to us.

As I have already stated, standing in front of the mirror is not a pretty sight for some of us. Even the most attractive among us can see some things that we do not like when we have shed our coverings. We need to understand that the Lord always sees us without our covering and God still loves us. Even when we are at our best in church praising his name and being our best selves, the Lord still sees us without our covering. Even when we have spent extra time getting dressed so that we can look our best, the Lord still sees us without our covering. Even when we are praying desperately and making all kinds of promises to God that we may someday break, the Lord sees us without our covering before the words leave our mouths. And yet God continues to love us and see worth in us.

A number of us are familiar with the story of the Emperor's clothes. The story is told of an emperor who so wanted an impressive new outfit, he fell victim to two shyster tailors. These tailors told him they were going to make him an outfit with special thread and cloth that only those who were loyal to him could see. If persons did not see the clothes it meant they were not loyal to him. The tailors brought back the imaginary outfit and supposedly dressed the emperor in it. Of course he was standing there naked but everybody was afraid to speak up because to do so meant they were not loyal to the king and would be considered traitors. Those in the court were so complimentary of the king he decided to march in a parade so everybody could see his new clothes. As the king walked through the streets of the town, all of his subjects bowed and "oohed" and "aahed" at his new outfit. Everything was going fine until a little boy who did not know what was going on and who could not possibly have been a traitor spoke up and said, "The emperor has no clothes." Word began to circulate in the crowd that the issue was not their loyalty and their eyesight. The emperor really was naked.

Many of us have wrapped our self-worth in the trappings of this world that has left us naked and vulnerable. We have defined ourselves by what we wear, what we drive, where we live, and what we do. We have defined ourselves by the negative things our enemies say and write about us. We have defined ourselves by the expectations of others and by our professional associations and various social clubs. We have defined ourselves by our titles and our jobs. We have defined ourselves by our relationships and by our family name or our marital status. Some of us have even defined ourselves by some astrological sign of the zodiac. We have defined ourselves by our guilt and our shame. We have defined ourselves by our faults and our failures.

However all of these definitions have left us naked and exposed to the vicissitudes and humiliations of life. What do you do, when like Job, you're on top of the world one day and overnight all that you have worked for seems to be on the verge of collapse? What do you do, when like Naomi, death claims the people you have loved and built your life around and you have to rediscover who you are now that the loved one is gone or now that the children have left the house and are on their own? What do you do, when like Elijah, in spite of the goodness of God in your life, the threats from the Jezebels in your life have struck fear into your heart and you are in a panic mode? What do you do when like the three Hebrew boys, your employer or boss has threatened you if you do not bow down to his or her demands?

What do you do, when like Daniel, a conspiracy by those who are jealous of where you are or who feel that you should not be where you are, have landed you in a lion's den? What do you do, when like the Samaritan woman, you find yourself isolated and treated like a social pariah and leper? What do you do, when like the apostle Paul, you have a thorn in the flesh and you have prayed and fasted and the thorn remains? What do you do, when like the Lord Jesus, you are facing Calvary with all of its pain and suffering, and prayer does not take Calvary away? What do you do, when like the Lord Jesus, you are at Calvary and your enemies are mocking and God seems to have forsaken you?

At such times we feel weak and exposed, naked and vulnerable to the outside world. With all that what we have, with all of that we own, in spite all of those we know, we feel worthless and ashamed as we discover that our self-worth and image and reputations have no clothes. Our faith has no clothes. Our significant relationships have no clothes. Our friendships have no clothes. Our financial security has no clothes. The good news I bring is that I know somebody whose name is Jesus, who sees us as we are and draws us to him and covers us with his righteousness, his love, his forgiveness, his cleansing and his power and gives us a new understanding of our self-worth. For, "if anyone is in Christ, there is a new creation: everything old has passed away; see, everything has become new (II Corinthians 5: 17)."

BREAKING FINANCIAL BARRIERS

It's Time To Take Control!

TEXT: LUKE 15: 17-19 and I JOHN 4: 4

When I was a teenager my father began to teach me how to drive an automobile. He owned a 1959 Dodge Royal Lancer, which was a huge car. What I remember most about it was it's long fishtail fins in the back. As a young student driver I was very nervous to begin with, but handling of the size car we had was also not the easiest feat for me. The car was so big and bulky I really had a hard time controlling it and keeping it on the track. After swerving a couple of times and commenting that the car was so hard to control because it was so big, my father finally said to me, "William, this car is going just where you point it. If you point it to the left it will go to the left and if you point it to the right it will go to the right. You are the one doing the driving; the car is not driving itself. You control the speed and you control the direction in which it is going."

There are times when we all feel that certain situations have gotten out of hand, and that we are being controlled by forces beyond our control. While there are certain situations that may be beyond our control and certain things that may happen to us that we cannot do anything about, I would caution us about relinquishing total control of our life, even to circumstances that are beyond our control. We cannot control what happens to us but we can control how we react to things that happen to us. There is the story of two soldiers coming home from the war and both had had their legs amputated. They began to talk about their plans for the rest of their lives. One soldier said, "I plan to sit around for the rest of my life and collect my disability and take it easy.'" The other said, "I am not going to let my not having legs stop me from accomplishing my goals. I always wanted to .go to school and learn computer programming. My injury will not stop me from doing either but affords me more time to do them both." Two men in the exact same situation, and yet their responses are totally different. I repeat, what happens to us is not as important as how we react to it. We cannot stop people from being mean or racist or sexist or petty. We cannot make people like us or speak to us. However we can control how we react to them.

Someone else's being small minded and petty does not force us to be small and petty. If we are small and petty because some one else is small and petty, it is because we have chosen to react or become that way. Someone else, refusing to speak, his or her insistence on being mean and spiteful does not force us to act the same way. If we are vengeful and bitter or if we refuse to speak because of how someone treats us, the problem is not with them. We have made a conscious decision to respond to their unkindness, rudeness, and ignorance in a certain way. If the sight of someone is causing our mood to change and our spirit to become sour; if we can't speak about certain people without cursing, or if certain people cause us to act in ways that are not our best self, they are not making us do it and neither is the devil or any imp or demon. We have chosen to act or react in a particular way to certain people and certain situations. When we allow people to determine our actions or reactions, they do so not because they are more powerful in and of themselves, or because they are superior. We have simply relinquished control of our emotions, and have put ourselves under their authority. Nobody can force us to act ignorant, or uncouth or unsaved. If being around certain people seems to bring out the worst in us, or if the sight or mention of certain people makes us depressed or angry, then we are out of control and it's time to take control. If working with certain people causes us to lose our joy or if a certain situation causes us to lose the joy we once had, then it is time to take back the control of our hearts, our minds, our moods, our personalities and our joy.

Let us never forget that we are in the driver's seat of our own minds and will— nobody else. We are driving how we act or react in certain situations. Our words will flow in the way that we drive them. Our moods will go in the direction that we drive them. Our life will go in the direction that we drive it. And our finances will go in the direction that we drive them. Let us not forget that when it comes to our finances we are in the driver's seat. We drove ourselves into the financial holes in which we find ourselves. We chose to max out the limits on our charge cards. We chose to buy what we could not afford or did not need, to keep up appearances or to keep up with someone else. We chose to buy now and pay later. We chose to spend rather than save and invest. We chose to assume debt that others made. When our expenses went up and our income either went down or remained the same, we made the decision not to make necessary adjustments to our lifestyle or spending habits. We chose to invest in depreciating rather than appreciating assets. We chose not to honor God first with our finances and give in obedience to the word of God regarding tithing, keeping ourselves under a curse. We chose to believe that the money or income we had at a certain time, the job we had at a certain time, or the political and social contacts we had at a certain time, or the resources we had at a certain time, we would always have and so there was no need to do better financial planning for the future. We chose to believe that we were young enough or secure enough or cute enough or indispensable enough to spend as if there was no tomorrow. With all of the newspapers, magazines, seminars, consultants, conferences and television shows devoted to personal finance, we chose to remain ignorant on financial issues.

Our finances went in the direction we drove them and the decision to point them in new directions is up to us. If we have either driven our finances off of the track or into a ditch or into the swamp, then it is time we take control of our financial vehicles. If we feel our finances are becoming unwieldy and we are not sure of where they are going, then it is time we take control of our financial vehicles. If we are not taking the best route to our financial goals, or if we need some directions or some gas to keep going to the place we would like to be, then it is time we take control of our financial vehicles. The good news of the text is that no matter where we find ourselves or in what situation we may be, we can begin to take control of our situation.

The familiar and much loved parable known as the Prodigal Son tells the story of a man who had two sons. The younger son requested his father give him that portion of the inheritance that would come to him in due time. The father complied with his son's request and the young man journeyed to a far country and began to live recklessly with the inheritance that had been given him. The word of God tells us that he "squandered his money in dissolute living. When he had spent everything, a severe famine took place in that country, and he began to be in need." He hired himself out to someone to feed pigs, which he would have never thought himself doing. When he was being raised in his father's house, attending the synagogue and the temple, and enjoying good times with his family and neighborhood friends, the thought never crossed his mind that one day he would be brought so low as to feed pigs. When he left home with money in his pocket and dreams in his head, the thought never crossed his mind that he would ever be brought so low as to feed pigs. When he was partying with people who were grinning in his face and helping him spend his inheritance, and telling him what a fine person he was, when his social calendar had more invitations to events than he could possibly attend, the thought never crossed his mind that he would one day feed pigs. With his education, his religious and social background, with all the people he knew and with all of those who grinned in his face when he had something to give them, the thought never crossed his mind that he would feed pigs.

One day he became so hungry that he thought about eating what he was feeding to the pigs when as the word says, "he came to himself and said, 'How many of my father's hired hands have bread enough and to spare, but here I am dying of hunger! I will get up and go to my father, and I will say to him, 'Father I have sinned against heaven and before you; I am no longer worthy to be called your son; treat me like one of your hired hands." At that moment in the hog pen, the young man made a decision to take control of his life. That is the Gospel of the Lord Jesus Christ, and that is why I never tire of proclaiming it. The Gospel of the Lord Jesus Christ is this—no matter who we are, no matter where we are, no matter how long we have been there, and no matter how we got there, we can still begin to take control of our situation. The hog pen, or the place where we are that is beneath who we are as the handiwork and creation of God, is not where we have to stay or end up. If the Prodigal Son can take control of his situation in a hog pen, without money, in a starving land, where no one is willing to offer him a helping hand, then we can take control of our situation also. However for us to take control of our situation there are some steps that are required.

First, we have to be dissatisfied with the hog pen. I imagine that when he was so hungry that he started to eat what he was feeding to the hogs, he had a eureka moment in which he stopped and looked around at where he was and looked at the dirty piece of slop that he was holding in his hand and about to eat. He asked himself, how did he as a fine young man who started off with so much in his pockets and so many dreams in his head get into this situation? How did he who had started so high fall so low? Have you ever been in such a situation of need, of brokenness of spirit, of depression and heartache, of confusion, of just plain sin and shame that you had to ask yourself, "How did I get to this place? How did I get into this mess? How did I get into this relationship or how did our relationship get to this place? How did our family get to this place? How did my career get to this place? How did my walk with God or my spirituality get to this place? How did I manage to drive into this swamp or land in this hog pen? What was I thinking when I made this turn, took this road or tried to take that curve going at that speed? What was I thinking about when I tried to run that light or what was I trying to prove when I kept on driving even though everything within me was telling me to pull over or stop or rest?" If you have ever asked yourself those kinds of question then you are not far from the kingdom, because dissatisfaction with your situation is the first step in taking control of your situation that you have driven incorrectly.

He then said to himself, "How many of my father's hired hands have bread enough and to spare, but here I am dying of hunger." The first step to taking control of our situation is dissatisfaction with our driving. The second step is to dream of a more desirable place. In other words we have to know that there is something better for us. Note what I said, we have to know that there is something better for us. I did not say that we have to think that something is better for us. I did not say that we have to wish that something were better for us. I did not even say that we have to believe that something is better for us. I said that we have to know that something is better for us.

As much as we know that we are a mess we have to know that we can be a miracle. As much as we know that our situation is bad we have to know that it can be better. As much as we know that our situation is better we also have to know that we have not reached our best. As much as we know that we are in bondage we have to know that we can have a breakthrough. As much as we know that we are in trouble, we have to know that we can triumph. As much as we know that we are broke, we have to know that we can be bountiful. As much as we know that we are in the mud we have to know that we can be on the mountain. As much as we know that we are with pigs we have to know that we can be with power. As much as we are a disgrace we have to know that we can be desirable. As much as we know that we are lonely we have to know that we can be and are worth loving. As much as we know that we have sinned, we have to know that we can have a second chance. As much we are know that we are detested, we have to know that we can be a delight. The young man said, "I will get up and go to my father..."

The first step in taking control is to become dissatisfied with the place where we are. The second step is to dream of a more desirable location. The third step is to decide to do something. The third step is to make a decision to take control. Many of us are dissatisfied and a number of still have some kind of dreams. The problem is that we never make the decision to act. For too many of us the time to take control of our situation is next week, or next month, or next year, or when we get ourselves together, or when our ships come in, or when the children go off to college, or when we get older, or when we get a raise or when we begin a new relationship or move to a new community or a new church. If the Prodigal Son could make a decision to take control, to take the wheel in his hands and start driving himself again rather than letting his passions drive him, in a hog pen then we can do it anywhere even right where we are right now.

So for any number of us, it's time to take control. It's time to take control of our homes. It's time to take control of our children. It's time to take control of our flesh and our desires. For our flesh cannot take us anywhere that we don't direct it. It's time to take control of our destructive habits. It's time to take control of our financial situation. It's time to take control of our career. People may take a job away but they cannot take away our options for life. If we are in the driver's seat then we can direct our career to more than one destination. "But when he came to himself he said, "How many of my father's hired hands have bread enough and to spare, but here I am dying of hunger! I will get up and go to my father, and I will say to him, 'Father, I have sinned against heaven and before you; I am no longer worthy to be called your son; treat me like one of your hired hands.' So he set off and went to his father." To begin to take control we must become dissatisfied with the place where we are, we must dream of a better place, we must decide to act, and then depart from the hogs.

As I have pointed out before when I have preached this passage, the Prodigal Son did not take any of the hogs in the pen with him. To get to the next level or dimension of living or our walk with the Lord, to get to the place of financial freedom, we have to say goodbye to the hogs. We may not only have to depart from some situations, we may have to separate ourselves from some people. If the young man had spent any time in the hog pen at all, he may have even gotten to know some of the hogs pretty well, their personalities and their eating habits. He may have even had one or two favorites or perhaps even given them pet names. Every one has some pet hog that we become fondly attached to either because we have been with it for so long, we have become accustomed to having it around, we've become accustomed to using it as our release and our crutch. However let us not forget that hogs are not equipped to journey with us to the place we are trying to reach. Therefore to keep our hogs we must stay in the pen with them. And so the choice that some of us are trying to make is between our favorite hog or freedom, our favorite hog or home, our favorite hog or the vision God has for our lives.

Not only did the young man have to leave the hogs he knew to return home, but also he had to do so without any definite commitment as to how he would be received. That is why he had prepared to tell his father that he was no longer to be called his son, but if he would just be looked upon as one of the hired hands he would be satisfied. The question is raised as to why should he journey the great distance home without any guarantee he would be accepted. The answer seems to be that any place in the vicinity of his father was better than where he was. The answer is that the journey itself led him away from the hog pen where his future was death at worst and bleak and mediocre at best. Sometimes we want God to guarantee success before we start the journey towards the vision God has for us. Sometimes we want God to assure us that we will not fail if we try. Sometimes we want God to guarantee we will reach what we strive to achieve. Sometimes we want God to guarantee we will not lose anything if we take risks.

The Prodigal Son however, shows us that sometimes we have to begin without the no-lose, no-stress; no-worries, no-tears and no-sleepless nights guarantee that we are looking for. Even though we have no guarantees we will achieve all that we are looking for, the journey is still worth it. Leaving our favorite hog is still worth it, because any where near where God wants to take us is infinitely better than where we are. No matter how good some of us have it, God is still able to take us places and give us blessings we never imagined. If we are in the hog pen any place is better than there. If we are in the mud in debt, any place is better than there. If we are trying to outrun checks to the bank, any place is better than that. If we are trying to become free of habits that cause us to lose sleep at night, any place is better than there. If we are in the mud with hogs, if we are where we know we should not be, or if we are in places that are beneath us, any place is better than there.

Besides, simply making the journey, no matter what the outcome and no matter how we will be received, we are still getting away from where we were. No matter whether father or elder brother receive us or not, whether we are received as son or as hired hand or not, just making our way to the place where we know there is opportunity for our future, gets us away from the place where we were. When we are journeying home or to the place of opportunity of deliverance and a second chance we will have all kinds of questions, such as "What if I fail? What if they don't receive me? How am I going to make it if they don't accept me? How will I survive if this opportunity does not work out?" Well if you survived the hog pen, if you made it away from the hog pen, if you made it from where you started from, you can make it anywhere. When storms rise in your life, when attacks come from every hand, when enemies come like sharks to the place where you are because they think they smell your blood, just remember where you started from. When the enemy tells you that you will not survive, when you begin to think about all of the bad things that could happen, just remember where you started from. Just remember what you started with. Just remember where you came from.

If you can survive the hog pens, the attacks, the lies that have already been told about you, you can make it anywhere. If you can survive past betrayals, denials, and desertions, you can make it anywhere. If the hog pen did not kill you, if the last attack of the devil did not kill you, if the loss of a loved one did not kill you, you can make it anywhere. If the break up of the marriage or the relationship did not kill you, if the devil coming into your home did not kill you, if the devil trying destroy your child and your family did not kill you, you can make it anywhere. If that last bout with illness did not kill you, if that last season of rejection, persecution and crucifixion did not kill you, you can make it anywhere.

The Prodigal Son turned towards home and a second chance. However, the word of God tells us, "While he was still far off, his father saw him and was filled with compassion, he ran and put his arms around him and kissed him." Like you I rejoice in the ending, but there is one question that perplexes me. That question is how did a young man who was so depleted and drained himself and who was in a land gripped with so much famine that it could give him no sustenance, find the energy to walk all the way back home from the hog pen in the far country where he started from. Perhaps the answer is found in I John 4: 4, "Little children you are from God and have conquered them [the them refers to strange spirits that mislead the people of God]; for the one who is in you is greater than the one who is in the world." That is why we can take control— the one who is in us is greater than the one who is in the world. That is the reason we can come up out of the hog pen and make the long journey to freedom as we travel through a starving land that can offer us no sustenance— the one who is in us is greater than the one who is in the world.

That is the reason that we can stand and withstand the attacks of the enemy when they come at us from all directions—the one who is in us is greater than the one who is in the world. That is the reason that we can hold our heads up when gossip and scandal is printed in the papers, broadcast on the airwaves, believed by saints, and whispered about by so called friends—the one who is in us is greater than the one who is in the world. That is the reason that we can believe victory when life contradicts everything we stand for and victory seems a thousand light years away—greater is the one who is in us than the one who is in the world. That is the reason that no weapon formed against us shall prosper and every word of judgment that rises against us we shall refute—greater is the one who is in us than the one who is in the world. That is the reason that we can survive Calvary and emerge as pure gold—greater is the one who is in us, greater is God the Father who is in us, greater is Christ the Son who is in us, greater is the blessed Holy Spirit who is in us, than the one who is in the world.

Greater is God who looked into chaos and called everything to be that is, greater is God who kept Joseph from perishing in prison, greater is God who opened the way for Moses and the children of Israel at the Red Sea, greater is God who spoke to Elijah at Mt. Horeb, greater is God who walked with the three Hebrew boys in the fiery furnace, greater is God who locked the jaws of hungry lions for Daniel—greater is that same God who lives in us than the one who is in the world. Greater is the Christ who walked on water and calmed the raging sea, greater is the Christ who conquered every sickness, withstood every demon, and defied every grave, greater is the Christ who rose from the grave himself to stoop no more and who lives and reigns forever—greater is that same Christ who is in us, than the one who is in the world. Greater is the Holy Spirit who fell on the church on the Day of Pentecost with fresh wind, fire and new languages, greater is the power that shook the prison doors open for Paul and Silas as they prayed at midnight—greater is that same Holy Spirit who lives in us than the one who is in the world.

When we have God whom we have within us, we can look at financial barriers and any other kind of barrier that blocks God's vision for our lives, and take control.

BREAKING FINANCIAL BARRIERS

It Ain't The Money, It's The Management

TEXT: LUKE 15: 11-23

A number of us have heard the old saying " a fool and his [or her] money [are] soon parted." I would not say a number of us are fools but a number of us have what I call the Prodigal Son syndrome or problem, which was that of mismanagement of his resources or waste. The story or parable known as the Prodigal Son is about a young man who received an inheritance, mismanaged it, found himself in dire straits and then made a decision to return home. His father welcomed him with open arms even though his older brother who had stayed at home spurned him. Down through the years a number of preachers have beat up on the young man for leaving home, going away to a far country, wasting the inheritance that he had received from his father, and landing in a hog pen. I would assert however that this young man is no different than a number of us who are in debt and have money troubles not because we are bad people, we just have difficulty managing our resources.

I would assert there is nothing wrong with a young person or anyone else having vision, gathering whatever resources he or she can, and leaving the safety and security of home or comfort zone, to pursue their vision. When we think about it, that is what the Lord Jesus did. Jesus was the oldest child with a living mother and younger brothers and sisters when He left home to pursue the calling and explore the vision that God had for His life. When we think about it, a number of us have done the same thing. At some point we left the comfort of our familiar environment to pursue a vision for our lives. We either had the vision of a better life through marriage or a job or of education and we not only left to pursue it we made a decision not to return to the nest on a permanent basis. Once we left we made a decision to stay away unless it was for a short visit or we needed time to recoup from some situation so that we could leave again once we got ourselves together. Or, we returned because our loved ones needed us to take care of them or we had to take care of the family property or business.

This young man in his hopes and dreams, his intentions and his motivations was no different than most of us who leave home. As a matter of fact we look at young people as strange if they stay at home too long. We begin to wonder when they are going to leave or why they haven't left. We sometimes forget the young man in the text did not intend to end up in the hog pen anymore than some of us intended to end up in the financial messes we have gotten ourselves into. The young man did not intend to waste his inheritance any more than we intended to waste the money that we have worked so hard to earn. The young man was essentially not a bad person; he just had management issues. He did not know how to manage his inheritance and so he wasted it. Either we manage what we have well or we waste it.

I would submit to you that most of our money problems do not come from insufficient resources. Our problem is not that we do not have enough money; our problem has to do with the management of what we have. That is why contrary to what most of us think, more money will not solve our problems. If we cannot manage little, we will not be able to manage much. Some of us are deeper in debt, with higher salaries than we were when we had less money. Why, because the more we have, the more we spend. For many of us, "it ain't the money, it's the management."

If we are not able to afford the basic necessities of life, such as food, clothing and shelter, then we have a money problem. Many times we struggle with the necessities of life not because we do not have enough money, but because we choose to spend the money we have on other things. Many of us choose to drink up, smoke up, charge up, shop up, party up, gamble up and generally screw up what we should be applying to our daily and long term needs. Most of us are in debt not because of our needs but because of our wants. The problem is not the money; it's the management. That is the reason that God will not give us more no matter how much we beg and promise. God knows we cannot manage what God gives us, so God will not give us more to mismanage. We are not bad people we just have management issues. It ain't the money, it's the management.

The young man whom we call the Prodigal Son landed in trouble not because he was bad or because he was incompetent he just had management issues. The young man whom we traditionally call Prodigal, whom I am more inclined to call average or just like most of us, ended up in trouble because he made several mistakes, one of which he could not help. First he lacked maturity. When his father gave him his inheritance it was the first time he ever had that much money. All his life he lived on a fixed income or allowance. All his life he lived on income he could earn based upon whatever work he could do. Consequently when he received his inheritance he did not have the maturity to handle it.

I would submit to you that most of us know how to do without. We know how to live on less because we have no other choice if we are to survive. Our problem comes precisely when we achieve what we have been working for, and that is more. Our major problems start in trying to handle more. We know how to bear our burdens; our problem is managing our blessings. We know how to overcome obstacles; our problem is making the most of our opportunities. We know how to do without; we just don't know what to do with. If we are ever going to live according to the more that God desires to pour into our lives, and that God will pour into our lives when we are obedient to the word of God and have faith to follow the lead of God, one of the first things we need to understand is that the management of more is a learned skill. Whenever we have had less, we will not automatically know how to handle more. Learning how to manage more so we will maximize that more, is something that we do not know intuitively or naturally, it is a life skill that has to be learned.

Most of us are under the mistaken impression that we will automatically know how to handle more. After all we have done a pretty good job of surviving on the little we have had. We forget that everything in life we do, we had to learn how to do it. We had to learn how to talk. We had to learn how to walk. We had to learn how to use the toilet. We had to learn how to eat. We had to learn how to pray. We also have to learn how to manage more. That is the reason many athletes and other celebrities end up broke after having made so much money. That is why some people who hit the lottery or those who come into riches quickly end up in worse financial shape. They never learned how to manage more. They knew how to live on less, but not how to manage more. As we learn we make mistakes. One of the things we need to understand is that every money mistake we make is part of the learning process of managing more. The loan that you made you should not have made, the thing you bought you should not have bought, the investment you made you should not have made, are all part of your learning curve or your schooling in the management of more.

Consequently when you make a money mistake don't beat up on yourself, learn your lesson. The problem with many of us is that we don't learn money lessons like we learn other things. We keep making the same mistakes and persisting in the same habits over and over again. However, once you make the mistake, learn from it. Don't keep doing the same old financially entangling things over and over again. The richest person in the world has made a number of money mistakes, the difference between them and us is that they learned from their mistakes and did not keep repeating them. The key to a number of our financial breakthroughs is learning from our mistakes.

The young man in the text was not aware of his lack of maturity or his inability to handle more, so consequently he overestimated his inheritance. He thought it would go farther and last a lot longer than it did. While he held it in his hands his inheritance seemed unlimited. It seemed as if it would last forever and never run out. He did not realize how fast money could go and how quickly it could get away from him if he had no system of regulating it or preserving it. He had no system in place for either preserving or growing his inheritance, He thought his inheritance was so abundant he could do whatever he wanted to with it, buy whatever he wanted with it, spend it on whomever and whatever he wanted, and still have some left over. No inheritance is so abundant and so sufficient that it will last without a preservation plan.

Since we have not had to deal with more, our more often appears more than it actually is. Some of us can remember when we said that if we ever made a certain amount of money all of our money problems would be solved. The amount seemed much more in our heads than it actually was in terms of our own expanding and growing desires as well as the demands of life. If we had maintained our same level of living or if the cost of living had remained the same, perhaps that amount would have been sufficient. However between our expanding appetite for more and inflation, we have discovered that our resources do not go as far as we thought they would. When some of us got that last promotion we just knew that we would be doing a lot better financially, However because we did not have a preservation and growth plan in place, we can't even tell we got a pay raise and promotion.

Let us never forget that everything in life gets away from us without a preservation and growth plan. Our health will get away from us without a preservation and growth plan. Our marriages and relationships, our families and our children, will get away from us without a preservation and growth plan. Our jobs we had so much faith in, our careers we have sacrificed so much for, our businesses we have invested so much in, will get away from us and we will find ourselves out of work if we do not have plan to preserve our usefulness and grow our skills. Our religion and our faith will get away from us and prove inadequate to meet the demands of our ever changing lives if we do not have a plan to preserve them and grow them. We seek God's face and abide in God's presence so that we can preserve and grow our relationship with God. God gives us visions so we can preserve and grow our productivity. Likewise our finances and money and our other resources will get away from us without a preservation and growth plan for them.

There is a question that each of us needs to ask ourselves and that question is, "what is my preservation and growth plan for my finances?' A better question, since we are following the word and vision of God for our lives is, "What is God's preservation and growth plan for my finances?" The tithe is the foundation and cornerstone of God's preservation and growth plan for our finances. Tithing is about more than giving money to the church. Tithing is the foundation for the preservation and growth of our finances because when we place God first, when we give to God off of the top, we demonstrate our love for God, We also demonstrate our obedience to the word and vision of God as the first priorities of our lives and not our own self-serving agendas. As we honor God with the tithe, God in his graciousness helps us preserve and grow our finances. God said in His word, "I will rebuke the locust [or the devourer] for you, so that it will not destroy the produce of your soil; and the vine in your field shall not be barren, says the Lord of hosts." Someone has said that not having a plan is in itself a plan to fail. Without a preservation and growth plan, our money will get away from us.

Without a plan we spend money thoughtlessly. The Prodigal Son spent his money thoughtlessly. We may not throw our money away on wild parties but like the Prodigal Son, but we do spend it thoughtlessly. We thoughtlessly eat out more than we should during the week instead of eating some of the leftovers that are going bad in the freezer. We thoughtlessly buy a pair of shoes or a shirt or a CD or something else that we had not planned. We thoughtlessly put something on the charge and then forget we have to pay for it at the end of the month. By the time we finish dropping five dollars here or ten dollars there or several two dollars purchases that add up to ten, our money has gotten away from us. Now I am not advocating that we become penny pinchers, but I am reminding us that constant thoughtless, unbudgeted spending month after month will always result in our having more month than money. Without a plan money will constantly get away from us because it ain't the money, it's the management.

The young man in the text failed to learn managing more. He did not have a plan for preservation and growth and then he made wrong choices about people. The people he spent his money on were around to help when he had money but they could not be found when he did not have money and began to be in need. There will always be people who will be more than happy to relieve us of our money. They are known as takers and users. Many of us are in financial trouble because we make the wrong choices about people. We spend our money on those who are willing to take but not willing to give in return. In space there is something known as black holes which are large vacuums where things go in but do not come out. Some people are like black holes in our lives, They will suck and drain us of everything they can, but will never give or add anything to our lives.

The Lord would have me tell you to be careful about giving to people whom you only hear from when they need something. Be careful of people who are always trying to make us feel guilty when we say no. Be careful of people that always leave us feeling drained whenever we are in their presence. Be careful of people who always ask "What's in it for me?" before they offer to give us a helping hand. Be careful of people who want lobster when we are buying, but who offer us hamburgers when they are buying. No matter what their title whether Brother or Sister, Uncle or Aunt, Cousin or Friend, Son or Daughter, or Husband or Wife, such people are users and takers and black holes in our lives.

The young man's management practices landed him in a hog pen where he was struggling to survive. Has the management of our resources landed us in a place where we are struggling to survive? Have our management practices put us in a place of mediocrity where we cannot see God's vision for our lives due to the financial barriers and mud and hogs around us? The good news for the young man, and for us, is that the place where we are is not the place where we have to stay. The Bible tells us he was so desperate and hungry he would have gladly eaten the pods the hogs around him were eating, but he came to himself. He thought about the abundance that even the servants in his father's house had to eat, and he said to himself, "Enough is enough. I don't have to live this way. I can do better and live better than this. I will arise and go back home." The young man had the desire for a better life and made a decision to do what was necessary for him to get that better life, which for him meant returning home.

The first step towards financial wholeness is the desire for something more. Some of us have been in bondage for so long, some of us have lived with little or nothing for so long, the desire for something better has been aborted in our spirit. After all we come from generations of poor struggling people, of renters and not owners, of unwed mothers and irresponsible parents, of addicts, alcoholics and dropouts. We have accepted the place where we are as permanent and inescapable. However the Lord would have me tell you, never lose your desire for a better life No matter how long you have been where you are or the way you are; no matter how many hogs surround you, who have no vision for a better life; no matter how many generations of your family have lived in the pen of low self-esteem, low aim and ambition, never lose your desire for something better. No matter how impossible the odds, no matter how many the obstacles, no matter how high the hurdles, never lose your desire for something better. No matter how many prophets of doom tell you what you can't do; no matter how difficult the road to recovery and wholeness may be, never lose your desire for something better. No matter how many times you or others you know have tried and failed in the past, never lose your desire for something better.

As long as you have the desire, deliverance is possible. As long as you have the desire, God can help you. As long as you have the desire, miracles can happen. As long as you have the desire, visions can come. As long as you have the desire, the devil cannot defeat you, As long as you have the desire, there is hope for your situation. As long as you have the desire, the hog pen does not have to be your final destiny or ending point. Good management begins with the desire for a better life and for freedom. The young man however, not only had the desire for life beyond the hog pen where he was, he also made a decision to do something about his situation. He said, "I will arise. And go back home."

Good management begins with desire and then moves to the decision to do something about ones situation. Desire is good, but desire is not good enough to become financially free. We must decide to act on our desires. Desire without decision is like a child in the womb that never comes forth. Desire without decision is like music in one's soul that is never composed. Desire without decision is like love that is never expressed or a marriage proposal that is never given. Desire without decision is like help that is never given. Desire without decision is like a day that never dawns. Desire without decision is like a habit that is never kicked or an addiction that is never overcome.

Desire without decision is like salvation that is never attained because we simply heard about Jesus but never received him in our life as our own personal Lord and Savior, Desire without decision is like holiness and righteousness and the next level that is never attained because we never gave the Holy Spirit permission to have full control of our lives. Desire without decision is like having our spiritual growth stunted because we only attended church but never joined. Desire without decision like faith without works, is dead. Someone has said that the road to hell is paved with good intentions. Well, the road to hell is also paved without desires without decisions. We must not only desire change, we must act on that desire and decide to do whatever is necessary for change to take place.

The young man said, "I will arise and go back home and I will say to my Father, 'Father I have sinned against heaven and against you. I am not worthy to be called your son, treat me as one of your hired servants." To get his life back the young man had to retrace his steps and reorder his priorities without the guarantee of success. He did not know how he would be received. However he was determined to get out of the hog pen. Good management begins with desire that moves to decision and involves determination. For us to have better management of our finances, we are going to have to retrace our steps and rethink our priorities. When we rethink our priorities and retrace our steps we will need determination because we will probably make mistakes. The road to recovery, like the road to the hog pen; like the road to financial bondage; like the road to divorce court; like the road to addiction, is not mistake free. We will make mistakes when we try to move from the muddy ground of bad management to the solid ground of good management. That is why we need determination. So, when, not if but when, we fall and fail along the way, we will get back up and continue the journey home. The young man was prepared to be rejected; and in fact his older brother did reject him, however, he was still determined to return home.

According to the word of God, while he was approaching home his father saw him a long ways off and ran to meet him and threw his arms around him and kissed him. The son gave his little prepared speech, but his father told his servants, " Go quickly and bring a robe for his back, shoes for his feet and a ring for his finger. Bring him a robe of anointing, a ring of authority and shoes of acceptance. Bring him a robe of compassion a ring of conquering and shoes of change. Bring him a robe of deliverance, a ring of devotion and shoes of dependability. Bring him a robe of excellence, a ring of eternity and shoes of empowerment. Bring him a robe of faith, a ring of forgiveness and shoes of fortitude. Bring him a robe of grace, a ring of goodness and shoes of glory. Bring him a robe of health, a ring of healing and shoes of heaven. Bring him a robe of love, a ring of life, and shoes of longevity. Bring him a robe of mercy, a ring of miracles and shoes of majesty. Bring him a robe of prosperity, a ring of praise and shoes of power. Bring him a robe of redemption, a ring of righteousness and shoes of resurrection. Bring him a robe of salvation, a ring of strength and shoes for standing. Bring him a robe of transformation, a ring of testimony and shoes of tenderness. Bring him a robe of virtue, a ring of vision and shoes of victory. Bring him a robe of worship, a ring of worth and shoes of witnessing.

As the young man made his way home he was met by his father who was a deliverer, who gave him a robe, a ring and shoes. Good management begins with desire, moves to decision, is fortified by determination and in the end is restored by a deliverer. The good news that I bring is that as we make our way to our home of good management through all of our ups and downs, and risings and fallings, we have a deliverer named Jesus who stands looking for us on the balcony of mercy and forgiveness, expectation and love, like He did when He hung on Calvary one day looking over a lost world in need of salvation. And, when He sees us on our way home, He will meet us with a robe of welcome, a ring of well-being and shoes of "Well done."

BREAKING FINANCIAL BARRIERS

There Is Another Way

TEXTS: LUKE 15: 11-24 and I. KINGS 3: 3-15

The parable known to us as the Prodigal Son is that of a young man who was given an inheritance, wasted it and found himself in a hog pen. While in the hog pen he came to himself and remembered the abundance that was in his father's house. He made a decision to humble himself, return home, confess his waste and ask his father to take him back into the household as a hired servant. According to the parable, when the young man was yet a long ways from home, his father sees him and runs to meet him. The father throws his arms around his son, weeps tears of joy and kisses him. He then orders his servant to bring his son a robe, a ring and shoes. The father then proclaims a feast to celebrate his son's return. While we are grateful and are warmed by the father's love and forgiveness, the focus of this message is how to avoid the waste that landed the young man in the hog pen to begin with. There was another way for him to manage his inheritance other than the wasteful way he did.

Let us never forget that being a child of God means we have options and there is another way to live. There is another way besides debt. There is another way besides addiction. There is another way to handle our frustrations besides lashing out in anger and bitterness. There is another way besides welfare, poverty, low self esteem and low ambitions and expectations, and the mediocrity that have been in our family for generations. There is another way besides the get over spirit that we have either grown up with or grown into or accepted as the rule of law for our lives. There is another way besides fear and anxiety. There is another way besides the role of co-dependent, needy, misunderstood martyr or abused victim that we have lived for so long. There is another way besides progress and then falling back into the same patterns we have sought deliverance from. There is another way besides wasting our resources.

This is the Gospel or good news because the enemy wants us to believe that we have no other options and no other way than the bondage we know so well. Some of us stay in debt because we are convinced that debt is the only way we can have some of the things we desire. Some of us do not tithe because we are convinced we cannot afford to do so and pay our bills even when God has told us to test Him, prove Him and try Him regarding His faithfulness to us. Some of us are convinced that 10% is too much to give to God who has given us everything. Some of us stay where we are because we have believed the devils lie that we cannot get out or get beyond where we are, either because we are too old or because we are too young. Some of us have believed the lie that because we have tried and failed in the past there is no hope for us. Some of believe we have no options because nobody in our family has managed to escape from the downward spiral in which we are caught. Some of us have even believed in error that our suffering and poverty or "unwellness" is the will of God for our lives. Let us never forget God is not glorified through our poverty or our abuse or our oppression, our tears, our sorrow or our living beneath our privilege. God is glorified when God's people choose another way to live besides misery and poverty.

The young King Solomon demonstrates the fact that there is another way to live and manage our inheritance besides waste. When we look at the young King Solomon in I Kings 3, his position was similar to that of the Prodigal Son at the beginning of the parable. Like the Prodigal Son, the young King Solomon had been given an inheritance that he did not have the experience or maturity to manage. As a matter of fact, the inheritance of the young King Solomon was greater than that of the Prodigal Son in that Solomon was given the kingdom of his father David while the Prodigal Son only received the lesser portion of his father's wealth. However even though the inheritance of the Prodigal Son was less than that of the young King Solomon, what the Prodigal Son received was nevertheless enough for him to waste. It is true that we do not all start off with the same resources and inheritance. Some of us start off with a less dysfunctional family than others. I have lived long enough to know that all families have issues, and none of them, no matter how they may appear on the outside, is perfect. All families are dysfunctional at times because they are made up of us, and we are all dysfunctional at times. However, there are some families that are off the charts in terms of being dysfunctional. Some of us come from saved, Bible based families and some of us do not. In these crazy, mixed up times, a saved, morally stable, Bible based family is a definite asset. Some of us start off with certain advantages based upon race or gender according to the society or culture in which we live. Some of us start off with more financial advantages than others and some of us start off with greater physical challenges than others. Because we do not have the same advantages, we will have different challenges pursuing God's vision for our lives, and we will operate on different timetables. Some of us will blossom later than others.

The issue however is not what kind of inheritance we start off with but how we are managing whatever we have been given to work with? The Prodigal Son proves that we can mess up a lesser heritage like we can a greater heritage. The Prodigal Son landed in the hog pen not because he had less than Solomon but because he did not manage well whatever he had. He had management issues. His problem was not the money, but the management. Whatever he had or did not have, one thing was true, he had enough to mess up. We may not have all we might desire to start off with, but three things are sure. First we have something to work with. We would not even be here if God did not give us something to work with. God has never started anybody off with absolutely nothing. When we think about where some of us started, and what we have had to come through, the only explanation is that God gave us something to work with. When we think about all of the barriers that stood between us, and where we are now, the only explanation for our survival and our being blessed as we are is that God gave us something to work with. God gave us a brain that kept thinking when the enemy kept throwing roadblocks in our paths. God gave us a body with a reasonable portion of health and strength that kept functioning so we could do what we had to get done when we did not know how we were going to do it. God gave us people—preachers, teachers, saints, and supporters in unexpected places. God gave us praying grandmothers, aunts and uncles, who believed in us and prayed for us to compensate for false friends, other dysfunctional relatives and jealous enemies. God gave us knees that kept on bending in prayer when we did not know what to do or when the enemy came in like a flood. God gave us the church to encourage our spirits when we felt like giving up. God gave us the Gospel; God gave us good news during tough times that reminded us of how much He loved us.

Secondly, whatever we have is enough to mess up if we do not manage it well. Many of us are not farther in life not because we do not have Solomon's greater inheritance, we are not farther along because like the Prodigal Son we are mismanaging whatever lesser inheritance we have. Third, whatever little we have to start off with is enough for God to do something and work a miracle with. Instead of complaining about what we do not have, we need to remember that even with all that we may not have we still have enough for God to work with and do something with. When Booker T. Washington invited George Washington Carver to leave his position as the first African American faculty member at Iowa State College and come to Tuskegee University in Alabama to become the school's director of Agriculture, Dr. Washington said in his letter, "I cannot offer you money, position, or fame. The first two you have. The last from the position you now occupy you will no doubt achieve. These things I now ask you to give up. I offer you in their place: work... hard, hard work, the task of bringing a people from degradation, poverty and waste to full manhood. Your department exists only on paper and your laboratory will have to be in your head." Dr. George Washington Carver did not have very much to start off with, but what he had was enough for God to work miracles with.

"Can anything good come out of Nazareth?" That was the question asked about Jesus and His hometown. When one looks at how He started in an animal grotto, with an animal-feeding trough for His crib He did not have much to start off with. However because He yielded His life totally and completely to His Father's will, God has worked the greatest miracle of all with it. God used that life to save an entire world and thus has raised His name higher than any other name, that at the name of Jesus every knee shall bow and every tongue shall confess that Jesus Christ is Lord to the glory of God the Father. The question we have to decide is whether we will be like the Prodigal Son who mismanaged and wasted what he had or whether we will be like Solomon who chose a way other than waste to live and manage what he had. Are you young Solomon or are you the Prodigal Son?"

What were the keys to Solomon avoiding the waste of the Prodigal Son? What was the way the young Solomon chose that prevented him from wasting his inheritance? According to the text, "Solomon loved the Lord, walking in the statutes of his father David; only, he sacrificed and offered incense at the high places. The king went to Gibeon to sacrifice there, for that was the principal high place; Solomon used to offer a thousand burnt offerings on that altar. At Gibeon the Lord appeared to Solomon in a dream by night; and God said, "Ask what I should give you."

Young Solomon was a worshipper. Young Solomon loved the Lord. Young Solomon sought the face of God. Even though his walk and his worship were not perfect, Solomon had a heart for the Lord. Young Solomon stayed focused on God. Young Solomon walked in a way that honored whatever inheritance he received. Young Solomon's love for God moved him to give abundantly to God without the expectation of receiving more. Young Solomon gave just because... When you truly love someone you don't need a special occasion to give, you give just because... That's really the essence of sacrificial and unsolicited giving—we give just because... Because Solomon gave and worshipped so freely, God showed up without being solicited, just because...

The key to avoiding waste is to keep our focus on God. When we focus on God we don't have time to focus on what we don't have because we are in the face of sufficiency. When we are focusing on the sun, we don't have time to be worried about not having a flashlight. When we are focusing on the rainbow we don't have time to be worried about not having a crayon. When we are focusing on a waterfall we don't have time to be worried about a half full cup. When we focus on God we develop a grateful rather than a grouchy heart and an appreciative rather than an anxious heart. That's what the writer of that old hymn was talking about when he said,

> When waves of afflictions sweep over the soul,
> And sunlight is hidden from view,
> If ever you're tempted to fret or complain,
> Just think of His goodness to you.

Wasteful people are not worshipping people because when we abide in the presence of God, when we truly love God and focus on God, we become so appreciative, first for who God is and secondly for what God has poured into our lives, we dare not waste. Instead we seek to give, because God has so generously given to us. Evil people and stingy people, are not true worshippers because the giving of praise and worship and honor to God ought to release other chords of giving in our hearts. Lovely people are lovely people wherever they are. Encouraging people are encouraging people wherever they are. Giving people are giving people wherever they are. And evil people are evil people wherever they are. Sensitive people are sensitive people wherever they are. Cheap people are cheap people wherever they are. And wasteful people are wasteful people wherever they are. Worship, seeking God's face, abiding in the presence of God, giving to God, helps us walk in ways that honor and elevate our inheritance rather than diminish it.

When we focus on God, God will show up just because. That's what God did to Solomon. God came to Solomon just because and said, "Ask what I should give you." This is not the only incident where God showed up just because someone loved and focused on Him. There is no biblical record that Shadrach, Meshach and Abednego asked God to show up in the fiery furnace. But God showed up anyway and walked with them in the fire just because. Paul and Silas were in prison worshipping and praising God, and God showed up just because, and their chains fell off. John on Patmos declared, "[I was worshipping,] I was in the Spirit on the Lord's Day and I heard behind me a loud voice like a trumpet.. .Then I turned to see whose voice it was that spoke to me, and on turning I saw seven golden lamp stands, and in the midst of the lamp stands I saw one like the Son of Man, clothed with a long robe and with a golden sash around his chest." I repeat, when we focus on God, God will show up just because and keep on blessing so we dare not waste. God continues to bless and honor good management that focuses on Him. Some of us are witnesses that when we focus on God, God will show up in our situations without being asked, just because. Some of us can witness, "I tithed and gave by faith not knowing how I was going to make it and just when I needed a miracle, God showed up just because." Someone else can testify, "I tithed, I gave and I was not even looking for a blessing. One day God just showed up in my situation and blessed me far beyond my expectation, just because."

Jesus is a "just because" Savior. He came just because we needed to be delivered. He came just because we were lonely. He came just because we needed someone to believe in us so we could believe in ourselves. He came just because we needed someone to be faithful to us after others had broken our hearts. He came just because we needed to be picked up after others had put us down. He came so that neither death nor the devil would have the last word about our future or our destiny. He came just because we were afraid. He came just because we were living beneath our potential. He came just because we needed another chance. He came just because we were broken and needed to be fixed. He came just because we needed someone to love us when we were most unlovely. He came just because we needed a vision for our lives that was greater than any vision that we could have for ourselves or that others could have for us. He came just because we needed to be delivered from money and debt strongholds.

God came to Solomon just because and said, "Ask what I should give you." Solomon replied, "You have shown great and steadfast love to your servant my father David, because he walked before you in faithfulness, in righteousness, and in uprightness of heart toward you; and.. .you have given him a son to sit on his throne today. And now, O Lord my God, you have made your servant king in place of my father David, although I am only a little child; I do not know how to go out or come in. And your servant is in the midst of the people whom you have chosen, a great people, so numerous they cannot be numbered or counted. Give your servant therefore an understanding mind to govern your people, able to discern between good and evil; for who can govern this your great people?" The word of God tells us. "It pleased the Lord that Solomon had asked this. God said to him, 'Because you have asked this, and have not asked for yourself long life or riches, or for the life of your enemies, but have asked for yourself understanding to discern what is right. I now do according to your word. Indeed I give you a wise and discerning mind; no one like you has been before you and none like you shall arise after you. I give you also what you have 'not asked, both riches and honor all your life; no other king shall compare with you. If you will walk in my ways, keeping my statutes and my commandments, as your father David walked, then I will lengthen your life.'"

Solomon asked God for wisdom. If we would avoid the waste of the Prodigal Son, if we would make full and best use of the money and other resources God has given to us, we will need wisdom. There is much that glitters that is not gold, that if we were to invest in it, we would lose. There are many people who glitter but are not gold, and if we take a chance on them we will lose. We need wisdom. And what is wisdom? There are many definitions of wisdom but the simplest working definition that I can come up with is this—Wisdom is just plain old God given sense. That is why Solomon asked God for it, because wisdom comes from God. Wisdom does not come from books. There are many educated fools. Wisdom does not come just from experience. There are many people with experience who never seem to learn anything from their experience, but keep making the same mistakes over and over again. Wisdom does not always come from other people because other people can make errors. Wisdom comes from God and those to whom God gives wisdom.

I have a friend who prays, "God help me to see with your eyes, feel with your hands, love with your heart and respond in a way that glorifies you." That's what wisdom is. It is having God given or Godly or God's sense. It is seeing as God sees. It is hearing as God hears. It is feeling as God feels. And it is responding as God would respond. Therefore before we make money decisions we not only need good sense and good information, we need God sense. God sense sees farther than good sense. In 1879 the Methodists in Indiana were having their annual conference. The presiding bishop called on the president of the college where they were meeting to make remarks. The college president said, "I think we live in a very exciting age.... I believe we are coming into a time of great inventions. I believe, for example, that men will fly though the air like birds." The Bishop said, "This is heresy! The Bible says that flight is reserved for the angels. We will have no such talk here." After the conference the Bishop, whose name was Wright, went home to his two sons, Wilbur and Orville, who in later years became known as the inventors of the modern airplane. In 1870 the bishop may have had good sense but not God sense because he did not see far enough. God sense sees farther than what may appear to be good sense at the time. That is why God never gave up on some of us. Good sense may have dictated that we were down never to rise again. Good sense may have judged us to be lost and hopeless causes. Good sense may have said we were a bad or mediocre investment. But God sense saw farther and said we could be the salt of the earth, the light of the world, saints of the Most High God, a royal priesthood, a holy nation, a peculiar and chosen people so that we could proclaim the marvelous deeds of Him who called us out of darkness and into His marvelous light. If we would avoid waste we need wisdom or God sense and according to the scripture when we have God sense, God adds to what we already have. God will give us what we did not ask for. That is why the Lord told us: "Seek first the kingdom of God and his righteousness and all other things will be added to you." Some of us are witnesses that God not only adds, but God multiplies. Some of us are living in the season of God's multiplied blessings.

The word tells us, "Solomon awoke; it had been a dream. He came to Jerusalem where he stood before the ark of the covenant of the Lord. He offered up burnt offerings and offerings of well-being, and provided a feast for all his servants." Solomon worshipped, he received wisdom and then he blessed others. He added worth to others. If we would avoid waste we must not only worship and stay focused on God and we must not only have wisdom or God sense. We must also bless others and add worth to others. God has blessed us so that we might be a blessing to others. While it is true that God can just show up in our situation, it is also true that more often than not, God will use somebody to bless us. Our blessing will come through and by way of somebody else's hands. Often God uses others to bless us. That is why the Lord said, "Give and it shall be given unto you, good measure, shaken together, pressed down shall men pour into your lives." When God blesses us directly we are connected to God but when God uses others to bless us we are connected to each other. We rejoice not imply that prayer works, we rejoice that somebody prayed for us. In this dog eat dog world, blessing others and adding worth to their lives even as others have poured into ours, is another way to live.

That is why we are followers of Jesus because we believe there is another way. That is the way He taught saying, "You have heard of old.... But I say to you..." There is another way. How would we sum up the message of His life and His death and His resurrection, we could do it in four words, "There is another way." He came to a Samaritan woman who was full of shame because of her failed relationships and told her that there is another way to live besides being the subject of gossip and the object of men. He came to Zaccheus and told him that there is another way to live besides being a slave to money. He came to Legion and told him that there is another way to live besides being a victim to demons. He told a dying thief on the cross that there is another way to live besides getting over on people. He came to Saul of Tarsus on the Damascus Road and told him that there is another way to live besides narrowness and hatred. One day he died on a cross and rose again to show us that there is another way besides sin and death. One day He stepped on a cloud and went back to glory and one day He shall return again in the same manner that He left to take us home to be with him forever because for us there is another way. Whoever you are and whatever your situation is, the Lord Jesus would have me tell you that if you follow him, there is another way.

BREAKING FINANCIAL BARRIERS

Prospering God's Way

TEXT: II CHRONICLES 25: 5-10 and MATTHEW 4: 8-10

What do Oprah Winfrey, Michael Jordan, John H. Johnson, Bill Gates, Donald Trump, T. D. Jakes, Creflo Dollar and the heads of the world's illicit drug cartels all have in common? They all are extremely rich; most of them, if not all, are even billionaires. How do they all differ? They all became rich in a different way: Oprah Winfrey became rich in the entertainment industry; Michael Jordan through basketball; John H. Johnson in the publishing industry. Bill Gates acquired his wealth through the marketing of computer software; Donald Trump through developing real estate; T.D. Jakes and Creflo Dollar through serving God and ministering to the people of God. The leaders of drug cartels became rich through the illegal distribution of poison and death.

My point is a very simple one—we can prosper in any number of ways. That fact is another reason that we do not need to feel jealous of anyone that is prospering. No one has a monopoly or patent on prosperity. We do not need to try to copy what somebody else is doing or ask God why we did not get someone else's talent and their breaks. The land of prosperity is not reached by a single road but by a number of super highways. Many of those who travel the super highways to prosperity do not have great talent, just great drive, great discipline, and great marketing skills. After all, Frank Purdue became rich by marketing chickens; Ray Kroc by distributing hamburgers through a chain of stores known as McDonalds; Sam Walton by riding around the country in a red pick up truck, buying merchandise in bulk and setting up huge low frills big box stores known as Wal-Mart's. Orville Redenbacher became rich by marketing popcorn; Mary

K. Ash by organizing housewives as distributors of her cosmetic products. None of these persons were Rhodes Scholars, or great athletes or had great acting or performing talents. They did not have great oil holdings like Ross Perot nor were heirs to great fortunes like the Rockefellers or the Dupont's. They were plain people hard working people who knew how to market what they had to offer. Some people are even prospering with very little in terms of actual assets, just a computer and a web site.

I have some shocking news for a number of us. When we look at the many ways that people are becoming rich and the many different roads that lead to prosperity, we already have what we need to start on that road to prosperity. We do not need more capital or money. We do not need a sponsor. We do not need a partner or a companion who has the same vision that we have. We do not need good luck. I agree with the person who said, "The harder I work, the luckier I get." We do not need to come from a background of money or wealth. We do not need what someone else has in talent or skill. We do not need to wait until next year.

We do not even need to wait until we clear away our bills. Why work on just clearing away our bills and getting out of debt when we can use the same talent to work on getting rich? With as much of an accomplishment as getting out of debt is, I want to push some of us to go to another level. If you were smart enough, disciplined enough, talented enough, sacrificial enough, young enough, old enough, strong enough and anointed enough to clear up all of that bad consumer debt, you are also smart enough, talented enough, disciplined enough, sacrificial enough, young enough, old enough, strong enough and anointed enough to become rich. The same qualities that you have used to bring you this far and helped you to accomplish what you already have, can take you even farther. All we need to do is expand our vision a little broader and work a little harder towards wealth creation and not simply paying bills. In other words what I am suggesting is that our goal should be wealth accumulation and not simply getting out of consumer debt. Getting out of bad debt or consumer debt should simply be part of the plan or a step for a long-term vision of prosperity.

I repeat, paying bills and getting our of debt is not a goal but step two in the right direction of wealth accumulation. We have already established the formula for wealth accumulation: Honor

God! Eliminate Debt! Build Assets! Wealth is simply the accumulation of the right kind of appreciating assets. I would submit that if you have eliminated much of your bad consumer debt or even if you are on the road to debt elimination, you are already on the road to wealth accumulation. All you need to do is expand your vision a little bit and make wealth accumulation the goal and debt elimination not the goal but a step in the right direction of your long term goal of wealth and prosperity.

Our Lord told the parable of the demon that was exorcised from the body and began to wander in the waste places of life. When the demon could not find anyplace to rest, it returned to the life from which it had been driven and found it clean and empty. That demon then went out and found seven other demons and returned to the life of the person that was clean and empty and thus the latter state was worse than the former. If we have no other goal than an empty bill folder, the shopping demon will return, the frustration demon will return, and the sale demon will return. The insecurity demon, the got to have it now demon, the spending demon, the buy now and pay later demon, the keeping up with the Jones demon, and the fantasy demon, will all return, and we may find ourselves in deeper debt than when we started. However, if the spending demon returns and finds our life filled with wealth building activity, generated by a larger vision and some long term goals, there will be no room in our lives for him to get the kind of foothold that he needs to build another stronghold of financial bondage and bad consumer debt.

We do not need a high IQ. A number of people I have had the privilege of knowing are not very smart generally; they simply know how to focus on developing one thing really well and then market it. We do not need to be either younger or older than what we are right now. We already have everything we need right now to start on the road to wealth and prosperity. All we need is vision, passion and a disciplined and focus work ethic. If you really want to be rich, think about what you can do, not what you can't do, and what you have to work with, and then get to work. If you can cook well why can't you be the next Betty Crocker? If you like to tinker with computers, why can't you be the next Bill Gates? If you can make people laugh, why can't you be the next Bill Cosby? If you can fix hair why can't you be the next Madame C. J. Walker? If you can think, why can't you be an inventor or the discoverer of a revolutionary idea?

In a certain major corporation there was an employee who had a big, beautiful, spacious office and who was paid more money than most of the people who worked there and had all kinds of stock options and bonuses. One day a group of high-ranking executives demanded to see the CEO of the company to complain about this employee. With fire in their eyes they said that they worked long and hard and they never saw anything that this particular employee did. As a matter of fact they had just walked by his open door and saw him doing absolutely nothing. "What was he doing?" the boss said. They replied, "He is just relaxing in his chair, with his shoes off, looking out of the window and throwing a pencil up in the air." The CEO said, "Then for heaven's sake leave him alone. The last time he was doing that, he came up with an idea that saved this company hundreds of millions of dollars and thousands of jobs, including yours." There are people who even become rich by motivating other people to become rich. The shocking news that I bring to some of us is that we already have what we need to become rich, if we just work with what we have

As there are any number of ways to prosper legitimately, there are also a number of ways that we, as the people of God, do not need to tamper with. There are some roads to wealth that we as the people of God do not need to walk down. With us, the means and the ends, have to work together. There is a right way to prosper and there is a wrong way to prosper. As the leaders of the drug cartel remind us, the enemy or the devil also knows how to prosper those who serve him. That is what the third temptation that the Lord Jesus had to face was all about. According to the word of God, the devil took the Lord to a high mountain and showed him the kingdoms of the world with their entire splendor. He showed him the Middle East, with its oil reserves. He showed him the diamond and gold mines of South Africa. He showed him the Tanzanite of Tanzania. He showed him the gems of Brazil. He showed him the banking system of Switzerland. He showed him the technology and the business acumen of Japan. He showed him the manufacturing potential of China. He showed him the gold and silver reserves of the United States. Then he told the Lord, "The politics and the military might that controls all of this is under my control. I will give you all you see if you simply bow down and worship me." The devil makes the same offer to us. He says, "You don't have to stop coming church and giving God praise on Sunday. You don't have to give up your shout, your step, your anointing or your ministry. You can keep your title, your membership and your favorite seat in church. You can even tithe if you desire. I just ask that you worship me even if you keep up the appearances of belonging to God. As a matter of fact, I prefer that you do both because some of my most effective workers are those who worship me with their flesh and their heart, while pretending to belong to God."

However Jesus understood that compromise with the devil and worshipping Him was not the way for Him to prosper. Playing by the devils rules was not the way He wanted to live. Not being all that God would have Him to be was not the way He wanted to prosper. Lies and deceit, breaking promises and His word, as well as the hearts of people He cared about, so that He could have better cash flow or have more money and things was not the way He wanted to live. Betraying friendships and trusts to advance His career and to get ahead, was not the way that He wanted to live. Not being able to be at peace because of what He had to do and with whom He had to do it to get ahead, was not the way He wanted to live. Not being able to sleep at night and not being able to look at Himself in the mirror and not being able to receive a compliment without feeling like a hypocrite, was not the way He wanted to live. Being afraid that His past would catch up with Him, or always having to look over His shoulders was not the way He wanted to live. Having an ulcerated or sour stomach and always being up tight and under stress ready to snap at any moment, was not the way He wanted to live.

Being a terror to family and not having any real friends but just sponges, hangers on and leaches who were simply out to get what they could from Him, was not the way He wanted to live. Having no one who really cared for Him as a person was not the way He wanted to live. Not having a God pleasing and honoring life, was not the way He wanted to live. Being a person who had things but no substance and few values, was not the kind of person He wanted to be. Having to burn in hell eternally because of the pleasure of a few years of enjoyment was not the kind of person He wanted to be. Not being His own person and having His principles and conviction on the auction block for whoever offered the highest price, was not the kind of person he wanted to be.

Being able to be bought and sold and having to be in bondage to keep what He had, with no real integrity, was not the way He wanted to live.

When we choose God's way to prosper, and see others prospering faster, seemingly without our headaches and struggles, there will be times when we feel that we are losing or that we will not do as well as others may be doing who either follow Satan's ways or who are following their own devices. As a matter of fact one of Satan's most effective tricks is convincing us that his way is better. His way of getting things fast is better than God's way of doing things right even if they take longer. His way of getting and keeping a man or a woman by lying on our backs or our front is better than God's way of standing on our principles and our virtue. His way of short-term pleasure is better than God's way of long term gains.

However God's way of graciousness is better than the devils way of greed. God's way of truth is better than the devil's way of trickery. God's way of principle is better than the devil's way of politics. God's way of conviction is better than the devil's way of compromise. God's way of devotion is better than the devil's way of deceit. God's way of righteousness is better than the devil's way of ruthlessness. God's way of faithfulness is better than the devil's way of fighting. God's way of salvation is better than the devil's way of scheming. God's way of integrity is better than the devils way of instigation. God's way of prayer is better than the devil's way of plotting. God's way of bridge building is better than the devil's way of backbiting. God's way of giving is better than the devil's way of getting. God's way of virtue is better than the devil's way of vindictiveness. God's way of undergirding is better than the devil's way of undercutting. God's way of mercy is better than the devil's way of meanness. God's way of lifting is better than the devil's way of lying. God's way of trusting is better than the devil's way of tattling. God's way of guidance is better than the devil's way of gossip. God's way of standing is better than the devil's way of stooping.

When we would question as to whether we lose by doing things God's way or prospering God's way we need to remember the small incident found in II Chronicles 25. According to the word of God, King Amaziah of Judah made a decision to wage war against an ancient group of adversaries known as the Edomites.

However he did not have faith in the power of his own army so he hired mercenaries from another land as reinforcements. The word of God tells us that Amaziah's heart was only partly turned towards God. Whenever our hearts, our focus and our lives are not totally devoted to God and the glory of God, we will always feel the need for reinforcements. Whenever we feel that prosperity is about us, how smart and talented or wise we think we are, we will always feel the need for reinforcements. When our prayer, worship and devotional life are not as they should be, when our affections are not what they should be, when our tithing and giving are not what they should be, we will always feel the need for reinforcements. When our faith and commitment are not what they should be, we will always feel the need to prop up our vision with other reinforcements such as other peoples opinions who delight in keeping us in bondage and who are more than happy to do our thinking for us. When we know that our relationship with God is not what it should be we look for other reinforcements like the horoscope or good and bad luck charms or lucky number or with superstition. Or we will cling to a childlike faith that is pampered by an over simplistic Biblicism or a backwards and naive way of looking at the life and the world. What kind of reinforcements are we using to prop up a faith that should be standing on the promises of God?

As Amaziah prepared to do battle, a prophet came to him and told him the Lord was not pleased with his battle plan and that he was to go into battle alone because his victory was not in the reinforcements he had found on his own, or in the schemes of his own mind, but in the God of his salvation. Amaziah asked about the money he had spent in securing the services of the troops. Not to use them would be a tremendous waste. However the prophet told him, "The Lord is able to give you much more than this." In other words, when we prosper God's way, we may have to take some losses in terms of some of the things, the people and the plans in which we have invested. Some times we have to let some things that humans and life offer us go, so that we might gain and prosper in God's way according to God's timetable. Some offers we may have to turn down, because as the Lord discovered when Satan offered Him the kingdoms of the world, the price is too high to pay.

What we turned down and what God rejected was not what God wanted for us. It was tainted in a way that we did not know. It would cost us in a way that we did not conceive. It would have made us dependent upon others in a way that should only be reserved for God. It would have interfered or blocked God's more excellent way and vision for our lives. What men and women bestow, men and women can take back on a whim. However what God has for us will come to us no matter what men or women may say or do. Men and women can't stop what God has for us.

I once went to see someone who considered himself to be a political power for assistance. He offered to help me in any way he could. However after he made his offer he told me, "Whatever I do for you, I will expect to be paid ten times over." I said to myself right then, that I would never ask him for anything because I wasn't going to pay anybody ten times for a favor they did for me. I was not going to be in bondage or slavery to anyone or be extorted by anyone for something they had done for me. I know that sometimes it is difficult to turn down some offers we see leading to prosperity. However before we submit to any offer that may come back to bite us, before we accept any offer from any snake, even if that snake is in Paradise, remember again the words of the prophet to Amaziah, "The Lord has much more to give you than this."

The Lord has much more to give you than the troops and weapons, the reinforcements that you see and are depending upon to deliver you but are costing you more than you really can afford to give. The Lord has much more to give you than the office or job or money that is coming with so many strings attached to it, and has an invisible strangle cord around your neck that you may not notice. The Lord has much more to offer than a temporary high and a few moments of pleasure. The Lord has much more to offer than a good time for a short while and guilt and shame for a long time to come. The Lord has much more to offer than money that is waved before you that will cost you your independence and your manhood and your womanhood and even your very soul. The Bible is right—What does it profit a person to gain the whole world and lose his or her very soul? (Mark 8: 36)

Before you respond to what you see in front of you, the Lord has much more to give you than this—this man or this woman, this grant or this money, or this opportunity that can turn out to be a nightmare. When Amaziah told the mercenaries he had hired without seeking God's direction because his relationship with God was so weak that he was afraid to trust God to give him the victory and prosper his plans, those troops became angry, and behind his back, attacked some of the cities in Amaziah's kingdom. When we turn down what others try to offer, which is not in the will or vision of God for us, and that will make us or keep us beholden to them, expect them to be angry and expect them to attack us to prove to us that we can't make it without them. Expect them to attack because our reliance on God means they will not be able to personally profit and use us for their own ends, like they were planning to do when they made themselves available to help us. Expect those whose help and resources we reject because they do not fit in with the word of God that we have received or the will of God for our victory, to attack our reputation and our credibility, our dreams, our careers and our faith. Note that the mercenaries did not attack Amaziah's main fighting force but some of the villages and towns that were in his kingdom. Expect attacks even upon those who are close to us and those who are under our covering or area of concern. If the enemy can't get to us, he or she or they will come after those who are close to us. However just remember that the same God who watches over us, who keeps us, and brings us through will also preserve those whom we love.

Further, the mercenaries did not let Amaziah know that they were planning to attack the other cities. They came against them with a surprise attack. Expect the enemy to come against us in places, through people and in ways we don't expect. The enemy specializes in the sneak attack. The enemy specializes in sniper attacks. When we hear lies told and believed by those who are supposed to be our friends and supporters and who ought to know us, that's a sneak attack. When we find ourselves under fire and can't figure out when the opposition is coming, where the rumor is coming from or where the investigation is coming from, that's a sneak attack. When stuff just happens out of the blue without warning and we find ourselves scratching our heads and asking, "Where did that come from?" that's a sneak attack. However let us remember that although sneak attacks may catch us by surprise, there are no sneak attacks when it comes to God. Consequently God will never allow a sneak attack to come without giving you what you need to endure it, to withstand it and to stand up under it. When attacks come either against us or those who are close to us, whether by surprise or not, because we give up what looks like much needed and powerful resources, when we turn down great offers, and those who made them come after us for doing so, just remember the word of the Lord, "The Lord will give you much more than this."

To break the financial barriers that block the vision God has for us that is greater than any vision that we can have for ourselves or that others can have for us, let us remember we are called to pursue the prosperity that God envisions for us in God's way. How do we know God's way? God's way is consistent with God's word. Tithing is consistent with God's word. Truthfulness is consistent with God's word. Faithfulness is consistent with God's word. Work is consistent with God's word. Sacrifice is consistent with God's word. Holiness is consistent with God's word. Treating people right and like we want to be treated is consistent with God's word. Trusting in God to do the rest when we have done our best is consistent with God's word. Obedience is consistent with God's word. No matter what the enemy offers, the Lord will give us much more than this if we obey His word.

The Lord Jesus knew this truth and that is why He turned down Satan and dismissed him. We must not simply turn down some things or some people; we must dismiss them as determining factors in our future. As was the case with Amaziah, the enemy came after the Lord with everything he had. Satan came after the Lord with betrayals, denials, and desertions among his own hand picked disciples. Satan came after the Lord with discouraging failure to understand his mission, on the part of those who were close to him. Satan came after the Lord with the powerful political collusion and coalitions between compromised religion and a corrupt state. Satan came after him with lies, physical torture and persecution, with pain and suffering. Satan came after him with a cross, which was designed to disgrace as well as destroy. Satan came after him with death and the grave that were supposed to hold him eternally.

But after Satan came after the Lord with everything he had, God came with what only heaven could give. God came with resurrection power that death and the grave would never touch again. God came with a name that is above every other name, that at the name of Jesus every knee shall bow and every tongue shall confess that Jesus Christ is Lord to the glory of God the Father. When we prosper God's way, God will give us much more than silver and gold, titles and position. "What no eye has seen, nor ear heard, nor the human heart conceived, what God has prepared for those who love him (I Corinthians 2: 9)." Paul told Timothy, " As for those who in the present age are rich, command them not to be haughty, or to set their hopes on the uncertainty of riches, but rather on God who richly provides us with everything for our enjoyment. They are to do good, to be rich in good works, generous, and ready to share, thus storing up for themselves the treasure of a good foundation for the future, so that they may take hold of the life that really is life. (Timothy 6: 17-19)."

BREAKING FINANCIAL BARRIERS

Don't Underestimate Your Small Steps

TEXT: HAGGA I2: 1-10

When astronaut Neal Armstrong stepped on the moon some years ago, the first human being to do so, he made the statement that has now become famous, "One small step for man, a giant step for mankind." The giant step for mankind or humankind that his small step represented was actually made up of a lot of small steps that humans had been making for centuries as they looked to the heavens and pondered if man could fly through the air like birds. The giant step for humankind was the landing on the moon represented the small steps of men fastening crude wings to their arms and leaping from high hills to the crude flying machines that crashed or fell apart before they took off, to the Kitty Hawk, the first airplane made by the Wright Brothers to make a short successful flight without crashing. Landing on the moon consisted of a lot of small steps by a number of forgotten people.

No matter what we are attempting to do—whether we are learning a new task or mastering a new body of knowledge, whether we are building a new relationship or a new life, whether we are pursuing the vision that God has shown us or whether we are engaged in the process of recovery from past hurt or past mistakes, we must never underestimate the importance of small steps. When we are involved in rebuilding our credit history or building a new financial future for ourselves, we must never underestimate the importance of small steps. Most of what we do in life is accomplished not by great bounds and leaps but by small steps. While we know this to be true, the reality is that taking small steps can sometimes be very frustrating. Taking small steps means that we make progress very slowly and a little bit at a time. The frustration comes because we see the vision, we see the goal, and because we are enthused about reaching the goal and the vision, or because we realize that time is winding up for us, or because we see others who are much farther ahead of us in terms of their own goals or in terms of where we would like to be, when we look at the small steps we have taken our progress seems so miniscule and paltry

Another discouraging factor about taking small steps is that a mistake can throw us back to square one or Jump Street, or can be devastating to any progress that we have made. When we are making giant leaps and strides and make a mistake, and are thrown several steps back, we can still see some progress from where we started. The momentum and the confidence from great leaps help us overcome our setbacks and mistakes. We feel that we can get back to where we fell or made the mistake with another leap or at least some adjustments or corrections before we take the leap. However it is hard to build up a sense of momentum and confidence with small faltering steps. When we have been making small steps, the time is doubled and tripled before we can get back to where we fell or made the mistake which makes reaching the goal or vision much more formidable if not impossible. It is much easier to give up when we encounter a setback with small steps then when we have been making great leaps and encounter a hurdle.

Another discouraging factor about taking small steps is that while we take them we often run across critics who don't appreciate our small steps and are quick to tell us about the progress we are not making and how far and impossible the goal is from where we are. When we are taking small steps it is difficult to stay encouraged when we are surrounded by "nay-sayers" and prophets of doom who tell us that we will never get to where we want to go at the rate we are going or who are always telling us about how many hurdles we have yet to overcome or who like to talk about days gone by or the good old days and how we will never at this season of our life be able to do what was done in times gone by. If we had gotten started earlier, if we had not made the mistakes that we have, if this were a different political or economic climate, or if people had religion or morals like they used to, if people were caring and would help each other out like they used to, then we may be able to reach our vision. However when we look at the way things are now, we will never be able to surpass what was done in the past.

How do you stay encouraged when we have to deal with the frustrations that are inherent in small steps to begin with and then have to contend with critics and faultfinders? How do we continue to work on getting out of debt and building a new financial future and becoming financially independent when our small steps do not seem to be getting us very far and then we are surrounded by people whose words are like weights upon our spirits that hinder and try to hold us down rather than helping us to soar? How do we overcome that mistake, that habit, that hurt and that pain from the past, when we are surrounded by those who don't believe we can do it and it's only a matter of time before we mess up or go backwards again? How do we stay committed in the midst of criticism? How do we stay focused in the midst of faultfinders? How do we stay devoted in the midst of discouragement? How do we stay positive in the midst of put-downs? How do we stay hopeful in the midst of hindering spirits? How do we continue to believe in the possibilities in the present when those who like to glorify the past surround us? How do we continue to believe in our future when all we hear is that the glory days are behind us?

How do we do stay encouraged when the negativism comes from people who are not necessarily enemies, but those in our own community, in our own family, among our own friends, among our own people, in our own household, in our own church, whom we would expect to be excited and supportive of us? However they just can't see or won't see the vision; they just don't believe that we can do what we know that God has shown us we can. Consequently they cannot appreciate the small steps we have made and so rather than encouraging us to keep making them they discourage us, they talk about us, they mock us, they laugh at us, they drain us of our joy?

Keeping a community and remnant of believers encouraged to keep taking small steps as they worked on rebuilding their lives and claiming a new future for themselves was the task that faced the prophet Haggai when he spoke the words of our text. When the people of God returned to the Promised Land of their heritage after living as slaves in the distant land of Babylon, they faced enormous tasks of restoring to fruitfulness and full productivity a land that had been ravaged by war and neglect. As they set about the task of rebuilding their individual lives, the temple, the house of God that had been built by Solomon during the height of his reign and their history, and that had been pillaged, vandalized, desecrated and burned when the Babylonians had invaded their country, continued to lay in ruins. They would get to it in time but they had so much other work to do, they did not have time or energy or resources to work on it at that time. The prophet Haggai however told them that their fortunes were tied up and bound to God and that they would not prosper financially or any other way when they neglected the God who they were counting on to bless and grant favor in the other areas of their lives.

Consequently if they expected to prosper they had to make God a priority and begin working on the restoration and rebuilding of the temple, the house of God. The temple that was in disrepair was the broken window in their lives, which if they did not repair it would allow their favor to continue to seep out and escape. I just need to point out again that when we take care of God, God will take care of us. When we take care of God by honoring God with our tithes and offerings, with our obedience to God's word, with our care for the things of God, the ministers of God, and the people of God, God will take care of us.

When we delight ourselves in the Lord, God will not only give us the desires of our hearts, God will also give us the desires of His heart. We know what we have in our hearts and we would be happy if God gives us what's in our hearts. However God has things in His heart that we have never thought about and never conceived. Some of us are in places and have gone places and have had experiences that we never thought we would have, we have met people we never thought we would meet not because we had them in our hearts but God had them in His heart. However to get what's in God's heart in addition to what's in our hearts we must first delight ourselves in God. When we focus on God, when we seek God's face and not God's hand, when we love God for who God is and not simply because of what God can do for us, God will give us what is in God's heart. When we make God's will and word our first priority, God who caused everything to be that is, God who speaks and worlds appear and stars begin to shine, God who is almighty, all powerful and all glorious, will open His heart and give us what we never even thought about receiving. However to receive the overflow that is in God's heart we must first open our hearts, holding nothing back to show that God is truly the first priority and love of our lives.

The prophet Haggai convinced Zerubbabel the governor of Judah and Joshua, the high priest that the future of the nation was bound to the rebuilding of the temple as sign and symbol of their devotion to God and their understanding that they could not expect God to fully bestow favor upon them while His house was in ruins. When the words of the text were spoken they had been working on the temple for about one month. In that one-month they had taken a small step towards rebuilding the house of God. They had taken a small step in demonstrating that God was a priority for their lives. They had taken a small step towards securing their financial future and the well being of their nation as they restored their spiritual foundation as symbolized by the temple. The word that came to the prophet Haggai one month after the work had been started on the temple also coincided with the Feast of Booths, which was one of the major Jewish holidays or festivals of the year. During this festival Jews would gather in Jerusalem from all over the land and naturally they would visit the site of the temple where the work was in process. Among those who saw the work were some who remembered the former temple built by Solomon in all of its glory. As they looked at excavation, the clean up that was going on, and the ruined condition of the temple that remained, they said that there would be no way for the new temple to come up to the glory of the old temple. Their words of criticism must have been very discouraging to those who were laboring under difficult circumstances to build for their generation, and in their time, a faith tradition to serve the people and the age in which they found themselves.

It is discouraging when you are trying to build a new life in the place and under the circumstances where you are, to have someone compare your situation to one that used to be or to another situation in another place and time and under different circumstances. Consequently the word of God came to Haggai and told him, "Speak now to Zerubbabel son of Shealtiel, governor of Judah, and to Joshua, son of Jehodazak, the high priest, and to the remnant of the people, and say, Who is left among you that saw this house in its former glory? How does it look to you now? Is it not in your sight as nothing? Yet now take courage, O Zerubbabel, says the Lord; take courage; O Joshua, son of the high priest; take courage, all you people of the lands, says the Lord; work, for I am with you, says the Lord of hosts, according to the promise that I made you when you came out of Egypt. My spirit abides among you: do not fear. For thus says the Lord of hosts: Once again, in a little while, I will shake the heavens and the earth and the sea and the dry land; and I will shake all the nations, so that the treasure of all nations shall come, and I will fill this house with splendor, says the Lord of hosts. The silver is mine, and the gold is mine, says the Lord of hosts. The latter splendor of this house shall be greater than the former, says the Lord of hosts; and in this place I will give prosperity, says the Lord of hosts."

These words can teach us three lessons about breaking financial barriers to vision. First, patience and time are needed when we are making small steps. It would take time and patience in restoring the temple from how it looked at that moment to how it would look when it was completed. After all it had lain in ruin for close to sixty years and what took sixty years to destroys would not be straightened out over night. The debt that some of us took years to create will not be wiped out overnight. The lifestyles and spending habits that led to our financial bondage have been part of us for years. The unhealthy ways that we have been taught to view both poverty as somehow more righteous and holy and wealth as somehow more tainted and less holy or evil, have been embedded in our minds for years. Suffering, doing without, and being satisfied with just enough to get by, have been ways of thinking for many of us for years. Money talk being worldly rather than legitimate religious conversation so that we can manage what God gives us and live without being beholden to unsaved people who have the money we need to fund the visions that God gives to us, has been an attitude that numbers of us have carried for years. "You can have this world, just give me Jesus," is a song that we have been singing for years forgetting that Jesus came into the world to challenge the hold of Satan in every sphere of the world where he exercises control so that we as the people of God can have life abundantly in the world as well as in heaven. Jesus never required us to give up the world for him. He required us to love Him first so that when He gives us the world we will know what to do with it and how to live in it so that we will glorify Him first in what He gives to us

When we begin to challenge and change some of our old ways of thinking so that our lives can be turned around in some new directions, we will do it in small steps and we will need time and patience. The problem is that we want God to undo in our lives overnight what has taken us years to mess up. Once God gives us a taste for freedom, and once God let's us see the possibility of freedom and a new life we want all of what God shows us to happen overnight. When we look at the small steps we are making and how far we have to journey to get to where God has shown us, we begin to feel that we will never get there. That's the lie Satan will tell us to keep us in bondage—we will never get there. That is the discouraging word that others who have lost their vision or never had one or who want to keep us under their control or with less than what they have will tell us—we will never get there. God does not show us anything that cannot be reached or attained with Him. If God showed it to us, the reason is that we can have it. Therefore be patient, it may take a little time, but you will get there. With God on your side, you will get there.

The people who were glorifying the former temple without appreciating the small steps that were being made on the new temple were "guess-timating" on what something would look like in the future based upon what it looked like at that moment in the present. However if there is one thing that 1 have discovered it is that we do not know how something or someone will look in the future based upon how they look in the present. We do not know how someone or something will turn out in the future when God starts working on them. Don't underestimate what God is able to do with temples that have been lying around in ruins, or that have been desecrated or that have been burned. Don't underestimate what God can do with lives and hearts, which others say are ruined, careers that have been burned, and relationships and bodies that have been desecrated. No one knows the new glory that God is able to bring from temples that have been overrun by the enemy.

Every now and then we may have to say to some people, "I may not look like much to you now. These small steps that I am taking may seem like they are going nowhere and that I am not making any progress. But you don't know how I will look and what new glory God is going to bring out of my life when God gets through with me. My career may not look like much now, but you don't know how my career is going to take off now that God has His hand upon it. Be careful how you treat me and laugh at me and talk about me now while I am taking these small steps. You don't know where God is going to take these small steps and how God is going to magnify these small steps to His glory. I know that I don't look like much to you now at my age. I know I don't look like much to you now at my size. I know I don't look like much to you with my habit. I know I don't look like much to you now in my poor financial condition. I know I don't look like much to you now with my background. But don't you underestimate what I can be, what I can do, how far I can go, what I can look like, now that God has charge of my life, now that I am following God's vision for my life, now that I have given myself over to the Lord Jesus, now that the Holy Spirit, the indwelling presence of God lives in me, now that I am believing the word and the promise of God. "

God told the prophet Haggai to tell Zerubbabel, the governor, Joshua, the high priest, and the remnant to take courage because he was with them. When we are trying to rebuild our lives whether financially, or emotionally or spiritually, and are being overwhelmed by the greatness of the task and the distance of the goal, when the small steps that we are taking seem so insignificant and we are feeling overwhelmed and discouraged, God has this word for us, "Take courage, I am with you according to the promise that I made to you when you came out of Egypt. My spirit abides among you; do not fear." In other words I am with you according go the promise I made to you when I picked you up, as we used to say, "out of the miry clay and set your feet on a rock to stay." I am with you according to the promise I made to you when I found you and set your feet on a street called Straight. I am with you to fulfill every promise that I made to you when you were in bondage and I told you that if you trust me with your life I would never leave you nor forsake you. I am with you according to the promise that I made to you when you were in the Egypt of your sorrow, the Egypt of your sin, the Egypt of your loneliness, the Egypt of your heartache and heartbreak, the Egypt of your regrets and your failures. I am with you according to the promise that I made to you when you were in Egypt, that if you trusted me enough to serve me, I would be your new master, I would take care of you, and feed you, and would be a fence all around you and that no weapon against you would prosper.

In verses 6 and 7 the words "take courage" come from God three times. When we begin to wonder if our work is in vain because our progress seems so small the word of faith says to us, "Take courage in the name of the Father. Take courage in the name of the Son. Take courage in the name of the Holy Spirit." Take courage because God will keep God's promises to us. Take courage because we are not alone. God has never broken a promise and God has never left anyone alone. When we are feeling forsaken and afraid, remember, God has never broken a promise and God has never left anyone alone. When others fail us, and comforters flee, remember God has never broken a promise and God has never left anyone alone. When we feel that our backs are up against a wall and we do not know where to turn or what to do, remember God has never broken a promise and God has never left anyone alone. When others disappoint us, lie to us, deceive us and betray us, don't give in to self-pity or bitterness, don't walk away from the vision or give up on the goal of excellence, remember God has never broken a promise and God has never left anyone alone.

When we are taking small steps we will need time and patience. When we are taking small steps remember that where we are now is not where we will end up because God has never broken a promise and God has never left anyone alone. Then remember this last word, "Thus says the Lord of hosts: once again, in a little while, I will shake the heavens and the earth and the sea and the dry land; and I will shake all the nations, so that the treasure of all nations shall come, and I will fill this house with splendor, says the Lord of hosts. The silver is mine, and the gold is mine, says he Lord of hosts. The latter splendor of this house shall be greater than the former, say the Lord of hosts; and in this place I will give prosperity, says the Lord of hosts." In other words, when we take small steps of faith and obedience, God will intervene in a new way and God will do for us what we cannot do for ourselves. The wealth, the power that others have thought belonged only to them, God will bring to us because the silver and the gold are His. God will cause us to prosper in places where we are supposed to fail. Some of us can witness that God will cause us to prosper and succeed and be blessed in places where others expected us to fail. God will bring gold out of grime, silver out of slime, miracles out of a mess, testimonies out of trouble, deliverance out of death, life out of lies, salvation out of scheming, strength out of sickness, power out of peril, creation out of chaos, conquest out of Calvary, Resurrection out of rejection, and Easter out of envy.

And the latter glory will be greater than the former. The reason that most of us do not experience the fullness of God is that we become stuck in former glory. We know that God has brought some of us a mighty long way. We know God has healed us from our diseases. We know God has answered our prayers. We know God has worked miracles and made ways out of no ways for us. However whatever God has done in our lives, is former glory. Our problem is that we are so grateful and awed by what God has done in the past; we stop looking for latter glory. That's why we stop growing. That's why we start talking about the good old days. We believe the former glory is the best or that it is all that we can expect from God. The word that comes to us from the text is that we have not seen God's best work in our lives yet. We may have seen God's mighty work, but we have not seen God's best work yet. There is some latter glory that we have not seen yet. That is why we have lived as long as we have; there is some latter glory God still wants us to see. That is why we were saved from that last mess that we were in and escaped that last close call—there is some latter glory God wants us to see. That may be the reason that we are in the storm we are in right now. We know how God delivered from storms in the past. But God wants to show us some latter glory in how we can be delivered from the storm we are in right now that we have never been in before.

That is why God has shown you the vision that he has—there is some latter glory God wants you to see. I don't know about you, but I am living for latter glory. I am grateful for all that the Lord has brought me through. But I happen to believe God is not through with my life so I am living and longing and pressing my way to see what latter glory God has in store for me. God has some latter glory for each of us. God has some miracles to surpass any that we have seen thus far. God has some worship experiences with him, that surpass any that we have seen thus far. God has some prosperity to pour into our lives that surpass any we have seen thus far. God has some anointing and some power to pour into our lives that surpass any we have seen thus far. God has some answers to prayers that surpass any we have seen thus far.

Whatever God has done in the past, God is not only able to do it again, God is able to out do God's self. Some persons can testify that just when they thought they had seen God do God's best work, God outdid God's self and went beyond their expectations. For the latter splendor of this house, of this life, of this church, of this vision, shall be greater than the former.

BREAKING FINANCIAL BARRIERS

A Heart Change

TEXT: PSALM 51: 10

He could hardly believe what he had done. He was the man after God's own heart. He was the man God had helped conquer the giant Goliath when he was still a lad. He was the man God had chosen over his older brothers to be Israel's second king after Saul. He was the man God had kept and given an army while he lived as an outlaw between promise and fulfillment while an insecure Saul sought in vain to take his life. He was the man God had placed on the throne of Israel after his season of wandering was over. He was the man with great skills as a musician, singer, and composer as well as great military prowess and political genius. He was the man who had been able to conquer the fortress of Jerusalem and had established the formidable Mt. Zion as its capital. He was the man who had moved the Ark of the Covenant to Jerusalem and had worshiped with such abandon that his wife was ashamed of him.

However, he had become involved in a disgraceful affair and had plotted the death of the husband of his lover because the sin he had committed in the dark was coming to light in an unexpected pregnancy. He thought his plan to conceal his wrongdoing had succeeded, until the prophet Nathan confronted him, and he had been convicted of his sin by the word of God. The text is David's psalm or song of repentance. After asking for mercy and cleansing, after confessing his transgression, after acknowledging the justice of God's judgment, after asking God to teach him wisdom and purge him of his sin, after asking God to hide his face from his sins and blot out his transgressions, David prayed, "Create in me a clean heart and put a new and right spirit within me." In this request David showed that he was looking for more than forgiveness, he desired formation. He wanted more than a second chance, he wanted God to create something entirely new inside of him. He wanted more than the mercy of God, he desired that God do something miraculous in his life. He wanted more than the situation straightened out, David himself wanted to be straightened out. No matter how chaotic your situation I know somebody who can bring newness and tightness to your life and His name is Jesus. If He was able to bring cleansing out of the cruelty of Calvary and if He was able to bring meaning out of the mess of Calvary, then it is no secret what He can do with your life. If He was able to bring salvation out of the slander of Calvary and if He was able to bring power out of the persecution of Calvary, then it is no secret what He can do with your life. If He was able to bring deliverance out of the destruction of Calvary and if He was able to bring resurrection out of the rejection of Calvary, then it is no secret what He can do with your life. Somebody may be saying that their life is not all that bad and they do not have all of that drama. If the Lord can work miracles out of the chaos of some of our lives, just think about what He can do and far He can take you and how much He can improve you when you have calm rather than chaos to work with. In other words, no matter who we are and what we have to work with, Jesus can give us a heart change that can take us to new places.

However for the Lord to do in our lives what needs to be done, we must surrender ourselves to Him. To get the best that a heart specialist can give us we must trust the skill of that doctor enough to follow His instructions and surrender ourselves to Him. We can't fight and second guess the heart specialist and follow our own mind and do whatever we want to do and then expect the skill of the heart specialist to work. The Lord Jesus is a skilled heart specialist. However if He is to do His best work with us, within us, and on us, we have to do our part. We have to surrender ourselves to Him. We have to follow Him even when we do not know where He is leading or what He is doing. We have to trust Him even when we can't trace Him. All He asks is that we surrender to the one who has been mending, fixing, replacing, and creating hearts for over two thousand years. He knows what He is doing. Jesus answers David's prayer like no other, "Create in me a clean heart, O God, and put a new and right spirit in me."

I recognize that there are times in which we find ourselves in trouble because we were treated unjustly. The politics around us would not allow us to stay where we were. I also understand that some of us can make mistakes so grievous we are changed in the process. I also understand that some events are so personally devastating to us, we are changed forever. The loss of a loved one, the loss of a skill or ability through sickness or an accident, the loss of a job, or the loss of a relationship through a bitter divorce or separation, the loss of our innocence or some of our naiveté or trust because someone took advantage of us, or other forms of loss, can change our personality forever. In those instances we need to pray that the heart change will be a good one and not a bad one. Some of us have had a change of heart but it is not for the better. Some of us have different hearts but they are bitter. Some of us have different hearts but they are so weighed down with guilt because we have not been able to forgive ourselves or because we have not been able to accept the forgiveness of others or of God or of Christ. Consequently, our different hearts are as vision blocking and as growth stifling as our old hearts. With many of us new is not better.

That is a point that we need to remember before we discard the old model. New is not necessarily better. That is why we need to pay close attention to David's prayer. He did not pray that God would create within him a different heart. He prayed that God would create within him a clean heart. He did not pray that God would put a different or even a new spirit within him. He prayed that God would put a new and right spirit within him. A right spirit is one that is grounded in the word of God. A right spirit is one that is filled with the Holy Spirit. A right spirit is one that is overcoming and not simply staying and stewing in anger and vengeance. A right spirit is a growing not a gnawing spirit. A right spirit is a wise spirit. A right spirit is a forgiven as well as a forgiving spirit. A right spirit is a spirit that is at peace because it has made peace with God and has the peace of Christ that passes all understanding. A right spirit is a spirit that has been bathed in prayer. A right spirit is a spirit that is generous but not foolish. A right spirit is one that is willing to live and let live. A right spirit is one that has been broken to the point that it has reached new breakthroughs. David prayed, "Create in me a clean heart and put a new and right spirit within me."

The Bible recognizes the heart as the seat of our desires, our drives and our passions. To illustrate the significance of the heart, let us use the analogy of a car. The mind is the computer technology or the buttons on the dashboard that keep us informed about the condition of the car—how much gas we have, how fast we are driving, whether or not our car is overheating, as well as the controls for adjusting the temperature as well as defogging the inside and defrosting the outside. The spirit in the car is the driver who wants to take the car to certain destinations at certain speeds by certain routes. The will power of the car is the foot on the pedal that determines how much gas or pressure is being applied at any given moment. The soul of the car is the manufacturer who puts his own special character into the life of the car. Some are built for speed, some are built for comfort, some are built for more rugged terrain, and some are built with sensitivity to ice and snow. Education or information is the gas that is put in the tank without which we go nowhere. Prayer is the oil that is the key for long life of the engine. Faith is the body or the shell of the car that holds the car together. Relationships are the gear mechanism of the car that can put us in such modes as drive, reverse, neutral, or park. However, everyone knows the heart of a car is its engine. No matter what other components a car has or does not have, and no matter what condition they may be in, when the engine dies so does the car.

As the engine is the heart of a car, so our own hearts are central to the functioning of the body. Someone has observed, "The heart is a hard-working marvel. It can keep on beating automatically even if all other nerves were severed. And, what a beat...it beats an average of 75 times a minute, forty million times a year, or two and a half billion times in a life span of 70 years. At each beat, the average adult heart discharges about four ounces of blood. This amounts to three thousand gallons a day or 650,000 gallons a year— enough to fill more than 81 tank cars of 8,000 gallons each. The heart does enough work in one hour to lift a 150-pound man to the top of a three -story building, enough energy in twelve hours to lift a 65-ton tank car one foot off the ground, or enough power in seventy years to lift the largest battleship afloat completely out of the water." [Tan, Encyclopedia of 7700 Illustrations, No. 2165, p. 542]

Consequently the Bible identifies the heart as the engine of the human spirit and soul. The fundamental tenet of the Jewish faith that serves as foundational to our own is this, "Hear, O Israel: The Lord is our God, the Lord alone. You shall love the Lord your God with all your heart, and with all your soul, and with all your might. Keep these words that I am commanding you today in your heart (Deuteronomy 6: 4-6)." Note the heart comes first. When Nehemiah received the vision of rebuilding the torn down walls of Jerusalem he talked about what God had put in his heart. David not only prayed that God would create within him a clean heart and put a new and right spirit within him, he also declared to God, "With my whole heart I seek you; do not let me stray from your commandments. I treasure your word in my heart, so that I may not sin against you (Psalm 119: 10-11)." The writer of Proverbs declared, "Keep your heart with all vigilance, for from it flows the springs of life (Proverbs 4: 23)." The prophet Ezekiel declared God's desire for his people, "A new heart I will give you, and a new spirit I will put within you; and I will remove from your body the heart of stone and give you a heart of flesh (Ezekiel 36: 26)."

The Lord Jesus said, "Blessed are the pure in heart, for they will see God (Matthew 5: 8)." In other words, the heart is so important that when it is right, we can see what no human eye can see and live because of the unbearable brilliance and power of divinity, we can look upon God in all of God's glory. The Lord Jesus said, "Do not lay up for yourselves treasures upon earth, where moth and rust consume and where thieves break in and steal; but store up for yourselves treasures in heaven, where neither moth nor rust consumes and where thieves do not break in and steal. For where your treasure is, there your heart will be also (Matthew 6: 19-21)." And where your heart is, your focus will be and your love will be. Where your heart is, your energy will be directed and your decisions will be guided. The Lord Jesus said, "The good person out of the good treasure of the heart produces good, and the evil person out of evil treasure produces evil; for it is out of the abundance of the heart that the mouth speaks (Luke 6: 45)."

Paul declared, "if you confess with your lips that Jesus is Lord and believe in your heart that God raised Him from the dead, you will be saved. For one believes with the heart and so is justified, and one confesses with the mouth and so is saved (Romans 10: 9-10)." Writer of Hebrews tells us, "Therefore, my friends, since we have confidence to enter the sanctuary by the blood of Jesus, by the new and living way that He opened for us through the curtain (that is, through His flesh), and since we have a great high priest over the house of God, let us approach with a true heart in full assurance of faith, with our hearts sprinkled clean from an evil conscience and our bodies washed with pure water (Hebrews 10: 19-22)."

In all, the Bible has 830 references to the heart; 505 references to the spirit; 458 references to the soul and 95 to the mind. Since the heart in the Bible is the seat of our passion, our worship and our commitment, our ability to do anything or overcome anything depends upon the impact something has upon our hearts. The story is told of a college student who had infantile paralysis and needed crutches to move around the campus. This crippled young man also had an unusual talent for friendliness and optimism and consequently was well loved and respected by his classmates. One day one of his fellow classmates asked him how he could always be so positive and encouraging to so many others. The young man replied that his ailment never touched his heart. No matter what happens to us, if is does not touch the heart we can overcome it in spirit. However if something or someone does infect and grip the heart they can become a stronghold to us if we are not careful. A number of us cannot go beyond where we are, we cannot reach the next level God wants us to go, we cannot break the financial or other barriers that block vision because we have allowed some things to infect and infiltrate our hearts.

We have allowed something that people or a certain person said or did to us, infect our hearts. We have allowed something bad that happened to us, to infect the hearts. That is why we can't worship or enjoy our blessings, as we should because we still are holding pain and anger in our hearts that has infected our hearts so deeply we cannot appreciate others for whatever gifts they may have. We forget that God may use them to bless us. Our attitude is that if the blessing comes from them, they can keep it. However, we don't reject a check that comes in the mail because we don't like the mailman. One of the ways that the Lord makes our enemies into footstools is by having our enemies bless us even with the stuff they meant to use against us.

We have allowed some mistake or some failure to infect the heart and now we are afraid to try anymore or to take any more risks or trust ourselves anymore or trust the word or vision we have received from the Lord. We ask, "What if I try and fail again?" Or we ask, "What if it does not work out again?" Well, the same thing will happen this time that happened after the last time we tried and failed. We survived, in spite of the embarrassment, in spite of the pain we felt, we still survived and we kept on living. God kept waking us up every day and giving us what we needed to make it day by day until we have reached the point where we are now. If God provided last time, if God helped us to make a new beginning last time, if God helped us work through our self-doubts, our confusion and our anger last time, God is still able and God is still faithful. God will help us do it again.

There are three P's that can infect our hearts and block God's financial vision for our lives. The first is the Poverty spirit. Some of us have allowed the poverty around us to get into our hearts and so we have a welfare and get over spirit. We don't know the difference between being broke and being poor. Being broke is a temporary condition. All we need is a penny in our pocket and that will stop us from being broke. However being poor is a permanent state of mind. Poverty is a condition of the heart that tells our minds to be content with little or nothing and that prosperity is for somebody else and not us. Poverty is a condition of poorness that has affected the heart so much that we are content to just survive and make do rather than live in abundance and overflow. Poverty can so infect the heart that it flows in some families from one generation to another.

The second P is the Possession spirit. A possession spirit is the spirit that causes us to accumulate more and more consumer debt as we charge things we do not need. A possession spirit is the spirit that infiltrates the heart so we buy more and more depreciating assets and other stuff rather than adopting a systematic savings and investment plan. A possession spirit is the spirit which causes us to buy things to keep up the appearance of success or to keep up with our neighbor or our sister or brother or other relative or somebody else that we feel we need to compete with and out do. A possession spirit is the spirit that makes us feel that the more possessions we have, the more stuff we have, the more successful we are. A possession spirit is the spirit of impatience that tells us that we have to have it now, rather than wait until later because we already have some priorities in place and are working on a wealth-accumulating plan of appreciating assets.

The third P is the pushover spirit that 'guilts' us into giving money to friends and relatives who give us sob stories even though we know we are being lied to, or even though we know that giving them anything is like pouring money and resources into a black hole into which everything goes and nothing comes out. A pushover spirit is when we go into our own retirement and savings account, or our family or children's' accounts, or jeopardize our own financial futures to bail out freeloading, sorry relatives and friends who always come back for more. A pushover spirit is a spirit that makes us an easy mark of those who are more than happy to relieve us of the money we have worked hard to earn. A pushover spirit is the spirit that makes us believe we are not being either loyal or supportive or a true friend or family member if we say the one two letter word that will do some folk more good than any amount of money that we can give them. That two letter word is "No."

When we allow any of the three P spirits to infiltrate our hearts we will not be able to break the financial barriers that block God's vision for our lives. For God is not going to pour blessings into the lives of those whose hearts are not ready to receive them. Rather, when the wrong spirit and the wrong priorities infiltrate our hearts we develop heart disease or malfunctioning hearts. We develop hearts that are enlarged with pride and arteries that are blocked with ego. We develop hearts that are enlarged with guilt and arteries that are blocked with shame. We develop hearts that are enlarged with bitterness and arteries that are blocked with anger. We develop hearts that are enlarged with insecurity and arteries that are blocked with stupidity. We develop hearts that are enlarged with present pleasure and arteries that are blocked with no vision for the future. We develop hearts that are enlarged with fear and arteries that are blocked with doubt. At such times we need to pray David's prayer, "Create in me a clean heart, O God, and put a new and right spirit in me."

The key to overcoming financial and any other barrier that blocks God's vision for our lives is a heart change that delights itself in God so that when God begins to pour out blessings into our lives our hearts will remain anchored in God. The key to our overcoming financial and any other barrier that blocks God's vision for our lives is a heart change that seeks first the kingdom of God and His righteousness knowing that all other things will be added to us. The key to our overcoming financial and other barriers that block God's vision for our lives is a heart change that gives us a new heart for God rather than for the things that we put so much heart into. The key to overcoming our temptations, the key to not turning back to the lifestyles and habits that got us into trouble in the first place is a new heart that gives us new character and new commitments, new faith and new force, new priorities and new power, new vision and new values, new worth and new worship.

"Create in me a clean heart, O God, and put a new and right spirit in me." David's plea indicated that he knew the source of the heart he needed. It was not in himself. It was not in his companions. It was not in his accomplishments or his army. It was not in his wealth or in his own wisdom. David knew the source of the heart that he needed, had to come from God. That's why he called on God to create a new heart for him. David had lived long enough to know that in this life no matter who we are or who we think we are, no matter how much power we think we have or how many people of influence we know, there are some things only God can do. There are some situations only God can get us out of. There are some doors only God can open. There are some blessings only God can bestow.

Notice David asked God to create a clean or new heart. In Genesis 1, God looked out over chaos and spoke forth an ordered and organized universe. When David wrote this Psalm his life was in a mess, and yet he knew that no matter how messy and chaotic his situation or life was at that moment, God was able to create a new heart and a new life out of the turmoil and trouble in which he found himself. The good news I enjoy proclaiming time and time again, is that I know a heart fixer and a mind regulator. I know the Great Physician who is a specialist at mending broken hearts and giving new hearts to those whose hearts have grown weary in the struggle for life. He declared one day, "Come to me all you who labor and are heavy laden and I will give you rest. Take my yoke upon you and learn of me, for I am weak and lowly and you shall find rest for your souls, for my yoke is easy and my burden is light... What makes your burden heavy is your trying to carry it by yourself. What makes my burden light is the fact that I am carrying it with you."

No matter how chaotic your situation I know somebody who can bring newness and tightness to your life and His name is

Jesus. If He was able to bring cleansing out of the cruelty of Calvary and if He was able to bring meaning out of the mess of Calvary, then it is no secret what he can do with your life. If He was able to bring salvation out of the slander of Calvary and if He was able to bring power out of the persecution of Calvary, then it is no secret what he can do with your life. If He was able to bring deliverance out of the destruction of Calvary and if He was able to bring resurrection out of the rejection of Calvary, then it is no secret what He can do with your life. Somebody may be saying that their life is not all that bad and they do not have all of that drama. If the Lord can work miracles out of the chaos of some of our lives, just think about what He can do and how far He can take you and how much He can improve you when you have calm rather than chaos to work with. In other words, no matter who we are and what we have to work with, Jesus can give us a heart change that can take us to new places.

However for the Lord to do in our lives what needs to be done, we must surrender ourselves to Him. To get the best that a heart specialist can give us we must trust the skill of that doctor enough to follow his instructions and surrender ourselves to Him. We can't fight and second guess the heart specialist and follow our own mind and do whatever we want to do and then expect the skill of the heart specialist to work. The Lord Jesus is a skilled heart specialist. However if he is to do His best work with us, within us, and on us, we have to do our part. We have to surrender ourselves to Him. We have to follow Him even when we do not know where He is leading or what He is doing. We have to trust him even when we can't trace him. All He asks is that we surrender to the one who has been mending, fixing, replacing, and creating hearts for over two thousand years. He knows what he is doing. Jesus answers David's prayer like no other, "Create in me a clean heart, O God, and put a new and right spirit in me."

BREAKING FINANCIAL BARRIERS

Heart Change (Pt. 2)

TEXT: PSALM 51: 1-10

Psalm 51 is David's prayer of repentance after his scandalous love affair had resulted in the death of the husband of his lover. In his prayer for God to create a clean heart in him and put a new and right spirit in him, David was asking God not only to forgive him but also to do something radically different within him. In that David asked God to give him a clean heart and a new and right spirit, David was asking God to make him over or anew from within. There is the story of an old man who used to pray every Sunday that the Lord would remove the cobwebs in his life. After hearing this man pray this same prayer for about fifty times, another member who just couldn't take it anymore yelled out, "Forget the cobwebs, kill the spider. Kill the spider that's making the cobwebs." David was not praying a cobweb prayer; he wanted God to do something about the spider that was making the cobwebs in his life. Thus he prayed, "Create in me a clean heart, O God, and put a new and right spirit in me."

I submit to you that before we can break the financial and other barriers that block God's vision for our lives, we need a heart change that gives us new passions and new priorities, new values and new visions, new accomplishments and new assessments. Persons who have been involved in or with heart surgery know that it is a very delicate and tedious process. A spiritual heart change that will lead to new thoughts in our heads and new actions with our hands and a new walk with our feet is not an overnight or hurried process. Creation is not instantaneous. God who has all power did not create the universe instantaneously. It was created over a series of days or over a period of time. Sometimes we want God to fix stuff in us and in our lives overnight that has been broken for years. We can join church in a moment, but it takes time to become a new creation. Joining the church does not make us into a new person. Joining the church just admits us into the hospital where the surgery can take place. It takes time for Dr. Jesus to perform surgery on hearts that have become diseased by debt, bloated by bills, and enlarged by excess. If we are to have a heart change that allows us to not only get out of debt but also move into a new season of wealth, there are several points I recommend we remember. If we are to have a heart change that honors God, eliminates debt and builds assets so that we can move into a new dimension of prosperity in all of its aspects—spiritual, mental, emotional, and physical, I would propose the following points for our consideration.

First we must always keep a long-term view before us. The reason we must keep the long-term view in front of us is that the heart sometimes resists change. The body has been known to resist and reject an implant or a transplant even though the old heart or organ was diseased or ineffective and needed to be replaced. One of the realities we must face is that when we try to improve our situation we will have resistance from our own hearts. We will have heartache that will feel like heartbreak. When our hearts, minds and spirits have been conditioned to certain behavior and particular ways of thinking, our hearts will ache and almost seem to break when we deny them what they have been accustomed to doing for comfort and to build self-esteem. The problem is complicated for some of us who come from families where certain patterns of thinking, living and acting have been transferred from generation to generation. Because we decide to honor God, eliminate debt and build assets does not mean that we will not be tempted to spend when we are frustrated or charge to keep up with the Joneses or buy when something is on sale whether we really need it or not.

Our hearts will ache when we say no to the temptation to charge and we feel we need something of comfort. There are some of us who have comfort pounds or comfort weight. That is weight that we have put on because we stuffed our face or ate when we were feeling frustrated or angry. We used food as a comfort and the added pounds are the price we paid for our comfort. Many of us have houses that are full of comfort stuff. Many of us have closets that are full of comfort clothes. Much of the debt we have is comfort debt that we accumulated because shopping gave us comfort. Buying now even if we had no idea or even if we fooled ourselves into believing that we would have it to pay later, gave us comfort. Some of us are driving comfort cars that we can hardly buy insurance for and put gas in. Some of us even live in comfort houses that we bought to prove to others and to ourselves that we have arrived, even though we are struggling to pay the mortgage. We cannot run with patience the race that is set before us looking to Jesus the author and finisher of our faith, with the damaged hearts that we have, it's heart surrendering time.

Some of us are even using the needs and wants of our children as comfort. We spend money we don't have so that our children can have what others have whether they need it or not or whether we can afford it or not. We feel guilty for not being able to give them what some other children have or we remember how we felt when our parents told us no because of financial reasons. Consequently we continue to dig ourselves deeper into financial holes so our children look as good as others in things whose value they may not know, to give us comfort. It is difficult and painful to tell our children no. Our hearts rebel against saying no to our children when their playmates and schoolmates come from homes that are financially stronger. However it is better that they experience short term embarrassment and be taught the financial facts such as honoring God and saving and investing, than develop long term warped attitudes because we are pretending to be what we are not.

Our constant juggling trying to make ends meet, our constant worry that something will happen to cause our house of financial cards to cave in, our constant worry that we will be discovered to be the financial phonies we are, is the price we pay for our comfort debt. Having children who are as messed up financially as we are because we failed to teach them sound financial principles is the price we pay for our comfort debt. We need to know that we can move from comfort debt to conquering debt. People who submit to major surgery have a long-term view. They have hopes of living a better life long term. They know there is risk with surgery. They know it is expensive. They know it is painful, that the recovery time can be awhile and that they will have to make major life style changes. Because they have a long-term view of life, they expose themselves to all of the risks, all of the expense, pain, discomfort, inconvenience and life-style changes. They believe that the quality of life they expect to have is worth the short-term sacrifices they have to go through to get it.

To break the financial barriers that block God's vision for our lives, we have to have a long-term view of our finances. I always encourage people to sit down and write some financial goals. Where do you want to be financially one year from now, three years from now, and five years from now? Write your goals down on a small piece of paper and make three copies of your goals—one for the Father, one for the Son, and one for the Holy Spirit. Keep one copy in your Bible and look at it everyday. Put another copy in a place in your home where you will see it every day—such as the refrigerator door, or on the mirror of the medicine cabinet or the mirror of your dresser. Then place the third copy in your wallet where you keep the cash or near your credit cards. When you are tempted to charge or buy something, have your long-range goals there to remind you of what you are trying to achieve. When your heart begins to ache because it misses old comfort spending habits, have your long range goals ready to remind you of why you are telling your heart no. Keep in mind the image of yourself as being financially free and independent so that when your heart begins to ache for some comfort spending, you can think about how you are trying to look, free of excess comfort spending pounds. When your heart begins to ache and almost break because you are denying it money for comfort by honoring God and building wealth through saving, investing and accumulating appreciating assets, pull out your financial goals and remind yourself of how you want to look and where you want to be in the long-term.

To have a successful heart change we need a long-term view and then we need to know that we are somebody and that we have worth without stuff. Much of our debt is due to our need for comfort and much of our debt is the need for self-esteem. We need to demonstrate that we are successful by the stuff that we have. We have to show our relatives that we are successful by the stuff that we have. We need to show our friends and colleagues that we are successful by the stuff that we have. We need to show our children that they are as good as others because they can wear the same designer labels stuff and go to the same stuff oriented schools as other children in our neighborhood or in our circle of friends. We need to prove to our enemies that we are successful and that we made it in spite of them by all of the stuff we have.

I was talking to a colleague in ministry and he was telling me about how well he was doing by talking about how much he was getting paid and how much he received for his anniversary. For him the sign of his success was stuff called money. He is like so many of us, who measure our self-worth and success in terms of dollars and cents, which allows us to get a lot of stuff. Some of us have our self-worth tied up into our title or our academic degree. We cannot tell you our names without telling you our title. We will forgive you quicker for forgetting our names than we will for not calling us by our title. Some of us measure ourselves by our position or our job or what we do for a living.

Some of us measure ourselves by who we know. Some of us get our sense of importance by the names we can drop and the people we know. Some of us measure ourselves by where we shop. No more Target or Wal-Mart for us, maybe every now and then we might slum at Costco's or B. J.'s, but for the most part we consider ourselves to be strictly full service and full price department store shoppers. We are beyond Macy's; we now shop at Nordstrom's or "Bloomies." We have moved beyond Zales and Whitehall, we now shop at Biddle, Banks and Bailey and Tiffany's. Meanwhile we are still renting or struggling to pay the mortgage. We are still leasing a car or praying that the car we own holds up. We are still outrunning checks to the bank or have credit cards that are maxed out. Meanwhile we are still losing sleep because we don't know how we are going to pay our bills. Meanwhile we are still about to be buried under the mountain of debt we have built. Now I want to be clear that I have no problem with stuff. I know what it is not to have stuff and 1 know what it is to have nice things—having stuff is a lot more fun than not having stuff. Having stuff is good and fun, but having stuff ought not determine our sense of self-worth. Some of us need to understand that we have worth and we have value and we are somebody worthwhile and worth being with and loving and giving the best to whether we have the right stuff or not. What applies to us also applies to others. If we don't have a lot of stuff but consider ourselves worthwhile without it, we should not expect others to have a lot of stuff to associate with us. In other words if we are a Mazda, don't require people to be a Mercedes to talk to us. If we are a cottage don't require other people to be a mansion to speak to us. What I am saying is that we have to understand that the value of others and ourselves is not found in stuff but in self.

We have value and have worth whether we are driving or walking, whether we are in Bally's or barefoot, or whether we can go on a cruise or not, or vacation whether others vacation or not. We have value whether we have a job or title or degree or not. We have value whether certain persons know our name or call our names or recognize our contributions or not. We have value whether we have two parents or not. We have value whether our parents were married when they had us or not. We have value whether we have children or whether we are in a relationship or not. We have value whether we came from the hill or the hood or whether we came from a mansion or a one-room efficiency. We have value whether somebody compliments us or not. We have value whether we are physically fit or sick and weak. We have value if nobody ever tells us how pretty or handsome, or how fine or how good we look. We have value whether others accept us, or speak to us, or desire to be with us, or want to be our friends. We have value whether others invite us to join their group or come to their party or their meeting or not. We have value whether we have a big church, or a big car, or a big house or not. We have value whether others think we are too old or too young or not.

We have value in and of ourselves. This is a point worth remembering because there will be times when our aching hearts will tell us we need to have certain stuff to affirm our success and who we are as a person. There will be times when our aching hearts will tell us that others will not think much of us if we don't have certain stuff or a certain brand of stuff. In those instances we have to know that we have value beyond the stuff we own. This message of self-worth is what we tell our children when we have to say no to some of their requests because we can't afford them. We tell them that we know they are disappointed and we wish we could give them what they are asking for. However they are not to feel inferior because they don't have and can't go and can't do what others may be able to do. They have value in and of themselves and their self-worth does not depend upon a certain brand or a certain trip or a certain team or a certain car or a certain group of friends.

The late Bishop James Parrot of the Lighthouse church of the Lord Jesus Christ in Newark, New Jersey, used to tell his children that he had given them his most valuable possession. He had given them the Parrot name. His father had the name before him and neither he nor his father had brought shame to that name. They were to take care of their family name just as he and his father had done. I once asked my son why he did not go to a certain school. He told me that he did not need to be known as a So-and -So man. He is a Watley. We need to know that without stuff we have worth because we have a name that gives us value—child of God, redeemed of the Lord, saints of the Most High, Christian, followers of the Lord Jesus Christ.

If I were to say names such as Simon Peter, John, James, Matthew, the apostle Paul, those who are members of the church would recognize these famous disciples and apostles. They were made famous by their association with Jesus. No matter what their past had been. No matter what mistakes they made. No matter what they owned or what they did not have. We know them by their association with Jesus. However lest we forget, when Jesus met them they were nobodies. And, if He had never come into their lives they would have died as nobodies. Consequently when He called them, died for them, forgave them, and entrusted His message to them, it was not because they had a lot of stuff. He called them, died for them, forgave them because of who they were in and of themselves and because of what they had to offer in and of themselves. When our hearts would ache for stuff to make us feel important we need to remember that the Lord Jesus Christ loves us for who we are and what we have in and of ourselves. At the end of the day, what will matter and give us standing in the halls of glory is not the stuff we use to affirm our self-worth but our relationship with the Savior. We have an identity apart from stuff and it is found in our relationship and walk with our Savior who loves us for who we are, and not for the stuff we have managed to collect.

When we have self-worth apart from stuff rooted in our relationship with the Savior it changes our relationship to the things we acquire. We understand that stuff is our servant and not our master. When we have self-wroth apart from stuff rooted in our relationship to a Savior we don't lose our souls, our heads or our minds over either the acquisition or the loss of stuff. We don't worship stuff but we use our stuff to glorify God. We have a vision of life beyond stuff. We don't get ourselves into deep holes of financial debt trying to get stuff because our first love is God. That is what seeking God's face is all about—loving God for who God is so that we have a heart for God and not for stuff.

To have a heart change we must develop a long-term view. We must know that we have self-worth beyond stuff. Then third, we must have faith enough to believe that God will give us the new heart we seek. With all of the risks involved with heart surgery, we have to believe the operation will be successful. We have to believe that the doctor knows what he or she is doing. We have to believe that the body will accept the new heart and that we will be able to live a better life. In order to have a heart change we have to believe that God will answer our prayer, "Create in me a clean heart, O God, and put a new and right spirit in me." No matter how long we have had the heart we have, God will answer our prayer for a new heart. No matter how many generations in our families have had the same heart of financial bondage, God will answer our prayer for a new heart. No matter how many of our friends around us have chosen to keep the heart they have, no matter how hurt we may be, God will answer our prayer for a new heart. No matter how many people tell us that we ought to keep the heart we have and that we are too old or too far-gone to get a new heart, God will answer our prayer for a new heart. No matter what the odds are against our getting a new heart, we have to believe God will answer our prayer, "Create in me a clean heart, O God, and put a new and right spirit in me."

The gospel of the Lord Jesus Christ is this—whoever you are, you can have a new heart. Your aching heart can be changed into an able heart. Your angry heart can be changed into an abundant heart. Your anxious heart can be changed into an anointed heart. Your bitter heart can be changed into a beautiful heart. Your broken heart can be changed into a bountiful heart. Your bruised heart can be changed into a believer's heart. Your cynical heart can be changed into a Christ-like heart. Your damaged heart can be changed into a delivered heart. Your disappointed heart can be changed into a delightful heart. Your empty heart can be changed into an empowered heart. Your fainting heart can be changed into a fearless heart. Your greedy heart can be changed into a generous heart. Your hurting heart can be changed into a healed heart. Your insecure heart can be changed into an inspired heart. Your jealous heart can be changed into a joyful heart. Your selfish heart can be changed into a sacrificial heart. Your sinful heart can be changed into a saved heart. Your tempestuous heart can be changed into a tender heart. Your worrying heart can be changed into a worshipping heart.

No matter what kind of heart you have, our prayer can be answered, "Create in me a clean heart, O God, and put a new and right spirit in me." It's heart-surrendering time. No matter how deep the damage, it's heart-surrendering time. We cannot cure or heal ourselves; it's heart-surrendering time. We cannot reach the next place the Lord desires to take us; we cannot reach the vision God has for our lives that is greater than any vision we can have for ourselves or that others can have for us with the damaged heart that we have. It's heart-surrendering time. We cannot mount up with wings like eagles, we cannot run without getting weary, we cannot walk without fainting with the damaged hearts we have. Our hearts cannot take the strain. It's heart-surrendering time. We cannot run with patience the race that is set before us looking to Jesus the author and finisher of our faith, with the damaged hearts that we have, it's heart surrendering time.

BREAKING FINANCIAL BARRIERS

'Til Death Do Us Part

TEXT: I KINGS 11:1-10

The topic as many of us are aware, expresses the intent of traditional marriage commitments. I believe that people should marry with the intent of making a lifelong commitment. Whenever someone asks me about writing their own vows or about participating in an ecumenical or interfaith ceremony I tell them that I have two requirements that must be included in any marriage ceremony that I am involved with. First, I only marry people in the name of the Father, the Son and the Holy Spirit. And secondly, the commitment has to be "till death do us part." Living in the real world as I do, I am aware that there are a number of couples that make that commitment but for one reason or another, they are not able to keep that particular vow. This is not a statement of judgment, but one of fact. Even though a number of marriages do not work out for any number of reasons, the intent at the outset was for a lifetime commitment.

If we are to break the financial barriers that block God's vision for our lives and walk in the blessing of prosperity and fullness, we need to understand at the outset that we are talking about permanent lifestyle change and lifetime commitments to live a certain way. As many of us work to eliminate debt and take charge of our financial situation, we need to understand that we are talking about more than a quick fix up; we are talking about a permanent fixture. Honoring God, eliminating debt, and building appreciating assets are not simply habits that we follow during a certain season or period of our lives, but are lifelong disciplines that we follow "til death do us part." Living within our means, the practice of giving God the first ten cents out of every dollar, saving the second ten percent, and living off of the other eighty cents, is not a simple light and trite way for managing our resources when we are trying to get out of debt, but a way of living that we follow "till death do us part."

When we decide that we will not charge anything that we can't pay for in thirty days, other than the necessary housing and transportation costs, and we will not buy what we really cannot afford so that we can keep up our status, appearance and image, or to keep up with somebody else, we are not talking about a temporary hiatus in the way we spend money. We are talking about a permanent halt that lasts "til death do us part." When we talk about saying "No!" to some things and people in the present, and living temporarily without some things and perhaps some people, because we have long term goals and a long term vision of financial independence, of being financially free, we are not simply talking about a passing inconvenience but a permanent commitment that lasts "til death do us part." When we talk about getting out of debt and staying out of debt, we are not talking about a stage of life but a standard of life that we will follow "til death do us part."

True financial freedom is not just about getting out of debt, cutting back on our spending, having some new priorities, managing money in a different way, for this season in our lives. True financial freedom means doing these things through all seasons of our lives, "til death do us part," whether we are currently poor or rich, young or old, or presently in debt or not. The problem with too many of us is that we do not mind doing stuff on a temporary basis or not doing certain things to get ourselves out of trouble or to solve a crisis. Our challenge is to continue doing or not doing what got us out of the crisis so that a new crisis does not emerge from the same old habits that got us into trouble to begin with. Many times we address the crisis with no intent of a permanent change. Our goal is to simply get out of the crisis so that we can breathe free again, and later return to what has proven to be destructive in the past and that puts us back into bondage. Many times our attitude is that, "I'll be glad when I reach my goal so that I can go back to doing certain things." Consequently we go on a diet by not eating certain foods and when we reach the desired weight and look, we celebrate our achievements by eating what put on the weight to begin with. Well, if something made us fat to begin with, if it proved to be bad for our health a few months or weeks ago, what makes us think that it won't have the same ill effect now that it had then?

Once we get out of debt, stay away from doing those things that put us in debt in the first place. Don't celebrate your financial freedom by going on a shopping spree and using your charge card again. Don't celebrate your financial freedom by stopping your savings and investing plan. Don't celebrate your financial freedom by cutting back on the tithe and other forms of giving, now that you have more money. Tithing is not about trying to get on God's good side so that God will help you get out of your tough situation. Tithing is about a lifelong commitment to honor God first and foremost with everything that we have and in everything that we do.

In other words many of us are specialists at patching but not instituting the permanent. If something breaks down or falls apart, we are good at patching it because patching is a cheaper short-term solution. We are less inclined to institute a permanent solution because we are looking at the costs associated with the permanent. However if we add the cost of all our short-term patches, we really haven't saved much in the long term because sooner or later we are going to have to seek a more permanent solution to what we have been patching all along. Consequently when we get into trouble we try to patch it up by church attendance, reading the Bible, more prayer, more wild promises about what we will never do again and by becoming more spiritual than Jesus. Because God is merciful God will rescue us and deliver us. Since we think our patch is doing the work, we feel we do not need to make any permanent changes to our behavior. We will just coast along until the next crisis, until the next leak in the relationship appears, until the next leak in our finances appears, until the next leak of trouble appears. At some point we need to wake up and recognize that what we need is a permanent solution and not simply a temporary patch. My point is that the discipline that yields to a lifestyle of financial freedom is about a lifetime commitment that says, "til death do us part."

As some of us begin to make changes to get beyond where we presently are, we should be reminded that we are going to have to stay with what we have started as long as we live, "til death do us part." true freedom, true transformation, true prosperity, true deliverance and true salvation are about permanence and not about patchwork. So if you have started growing for God's glory, stay with growth till death do you part, don't just grow to a certain point and stop. If you have started seeking God's face and abiding in the presence of God, stay with it 'til death do you part, and don't go back to seeking God only when you want something from God's blessing hand. If you have started worshipping God on a regular basis or attending church, stay with it 'til death do you part. Don't stop when things either start going good or bad during certain seasons in your life. If you have started tithing, stay with it 'tll death do you part. Don't stop tithing during those times when your money gets funny or when you begin to prosper so much that ten percent seems like a whole lot. If you have started saving and investing stay with it, 'til death do you part. Don't stop saving and investing once you get a certain amount, and because it is more than you have ever had, you conclude that you have enough. If you have started living within your means and only buying what you can really afford instead of building up credit card debt, stay with the policy ' tll death do you part. Don't stop because you can now have a larger credit line or because you don't have any debt.

If you have started telling the devil no, stay with that practice 'til death do you part. Don't stop because you have been clean or free or celibate or resisting temptation or eating healthy for a certain time, so now you celebrate by behavior that makes you more vulnerable to bondage again. If you have started trusting in God, trust 'til death do you part. Don't stop trusting God because things get rough or because God said no to your prayers or because God has allowed some things to happen that you do not understand. If you have started believing in your possibilities, keep believing in who you are in God, 'til death do you part. Don't stop because of the negative things you hear said about you and the discouraging things people say to you. Don't stop because the devil has gotten a temporary victory in your life. If you have started pursing the vision or visions that God has shown you, hold on to your visions' til death do you part. Don't forsake the vision because the enemy is trying to defeat it and you, or because some doors have been closed in your face. Remember, God is faithful. If you have been doing well or if you have become a giver, stay as you are 'til death do you part. Don't forsake goodness because your good is spoken of as evil or because some of those whom you thought were your friends turn on you. If you have started serving the Lord with everything that you have, stay with God till death do you part. Don't stop giving God praise and worship or glory because life gets rough and the devil gets busier. Continue to say like the Psalmist, "I will bless the Lord at all times; his praise shall continually be in my mouth. (Psalm 34: 1)"

If we fail to make commitments to change and grow 'til death do us part then we can end up like Solomon. When we look at the young Solomon he had truly been blessed and highly favored of the Lord. Like his father David, whom God had selected over his older brothers to become King of Israel, David had also promoted Solomon over some of his other siblings who thought that the reigns of power should come to them.

When the throne was bestowed upon Solomon, he followed his father's example of loving God and was so generous in expressing his thanksgiving that he offered a thousand burnt offerings on the altar. God was so moved at Solomon's expressions of praise and thanksgiving that God appeared to him in a dream and asked what the young fledgling king desired. At that time Solomon had a grateful heart and recognized God's unmerited favor. Consequently he asked God for a wise and discerning mind so that he would know how to govern God's people. God was pleased with Solomon's request and God said to him, "Because you have asked this, and have not asked for yourself long life or riches, or for the life of your enemies, but have asked for yourself understanding to do what is right, I now do according to your word. Indeed I give you a wise and discerning mind; no one like you has been before you and no one like you shall arise after you. I give you also what you have not asked, both riches and honor all your life; no other king shall compare with you. If you will walk in my ways, keeping my statutes and my commandments, as your father David walked, then I will lengthen your life." Due to the fact that David was a warrior king, and had fought so many battles before him, when Solomon came to the throne the major hostile neighbors surrounding him had already been subdued and thus Solomon had peace on all sides.

Let me just point out that while each of us ought to have our own battles to fight, there are some battles that should not be fought over and over again, from one generation to another. There are some enemies that we have no control over, and some we can conquer. Battles of poverty, and low underachievement and ambition should not be fought in every generation. There are too many curses of poverty, low ambition and underachievement that are fought in some families from generation to generation. Our job is to leave something of substance behind, to lay a foundation and to fight some battles so that the next generation can build thereon and will not contend with some of the same issues that tried to cripple us. If the next generation fails to walk in their privilege and opportunity, they have to answer for their own sins of short sightedness. Our job is to conquer some enemies like poverty, so that those who come after us will not have to face those foes in our families.

Solomon was privileged to build the temple that was denied his father. Because David was fighting battles that his son Solomon would not have to fight, David could not build the temple that his heart desired to build for God. David saw the vision, and David even provided many of the financial resources needed to do the work, but he could not build because he was so busy battling. It is possible for the enemy to have us so embroiled in so many battles that we are never able to build what we envision. However if we have laid the right foundation, then the vision will become a reality in the next generation. They will get the glory of building and we will get the glory of seeing the vision and laying the right kind of foundation so that the vision becomes reality.

According to the word of God, Solomon's influence and fame spread throughout the world, as he knew it. Even the famed African Queen of Sheba heard of Solomon and came to Jerusalem from the heart of Africa, the Mother Continent, to be blessed by his wisdom. When she visited with him, Solomon shared with her all of his wisdom. There was nothing that she asked that he did not share with her. She even observed the generous burnt offerings that he offered in worship, praise and thanksgiving to God. When the queen of Sheba had seen the way that God had blessed Solomon, she said, "The report was true that I heard in my own land of your accomplishments and of your wisdom, but I did not believe the reports until I came and my own eyes had seen it. Not even half had been told me; your wisdom and prosperity far surpass the report that I had heard. Happy are your wives! Happy are your servants, who continually attend you and hear your wisdom! Blessed be the Lord your God, who has delighted in you and set you on the throne of Israel! Because the Lord loved Israel forever, He has made you king to execute justice and righteousness."

The word of God went on to say, "Thus Solomon excelled all the kings of the earth in riches and in wisdom. The whole earth sought the presence of Solomon to hear his wisdom, which God had put into his mind. Every one of them brought a present, objects of silver and gold, garments, weaponry, spices, horses and mules, so much year by year." Under Solomon silver in Jerusalem was said to be as common as stones. The tenth chapter of I Kings ends with a glorious testimony of the wealth and the wisdom, the prosperity and the power, the devotion and the dynamism, the faithfulness and the finery of Solomon. When many of us think of Solomon we think of how he is described in chapter 10. However, Solomon's life does not end with chapter ten. The glory of Solomon described in chapter 10 does not tell the whole story of his life and his reign. Don't ever judge the worth or the future or the destiny or the success or the failure of somebody's life by how they look in any one chapter. Many a person has looked at a person when they were in a down chapter in their life and said they were finished and done with. They concluded that their lives and careers were over and that they would never recover from the way they looked in a certain chapter of their life. They felt they could talk to them in any way, say anything about them or to them, kick them and treat them in any kind of way because of how they looked in that chapter of their life.

There are still others who sold out their principles, their morals or convictions, their friendships and betrayed their trust because certain people in certain chapters of their lives seemed invincible and unstoppable. And there are those who felt that how they appear in a certain chapter is how they will always be. Consequently they felt free to walk on and walk over people according to the power or authority they had in a certain chapter of their lives. However a chapter is just that - a chapter and does not tell the whole story of somebody's life. And the story can end much differently than any one chapter concludes. We all need to be reminded that we can end up in a different place than where we are in this chapter in our life. How the story of your life ends can be much different than the way this chapter is turning out. If you are in an up chapter don't think too highly of yourself because God is still writing chapters in your life. And if you are in a down chapter don't think too little of yourself because God is still writing chapters in your life.

When we leave chapter 10 and begin chapter 11 we see another portrait of Solomon. Chapter 10 tells of Solomon's faithfulness, but chapter 11 talks about his fickleness. Chapter 10 tells of Solomon's favor but chapter 11 tells of his foolishness. Chapter 10 tells of Solomon's devotion, but chapter 11 talks about his desertion. Chapter 10 tells of Solomon's strengths but chapter 11 tells of his straying. Chapter 10 tells of Solomon's worship, but chapter 11 tells of his wildness. Chapter 10 tells of Solomon's wisdom, but chapter 11 tells of his weakness. Chapter 10 tells us of how Solomon loved the Lord, but chapter 11 tells us that he did not love the Lord until his death. According to verse 4, chapter 11, "...when Solomon was old, his wives turned away his heart after other gods; and his heart was not true to the Lord his God, as was the heart of his father David." The Bible goes on to say, "the Lord was angry with Solomon, because his heart had turned away from the Lord, the God of Israel, who had appeared to him twice, and had commanded him concerning this matter, that he should not follow other gods; but he did not observe what the Lord commanded. Therefore the Lord said to Solomon, "Since this has been your mind and you have not kept my covenant and my statues, that I have commended you, I will surely tear the kingdom from you and give it to your servant."

That was the last word that the scriptures record of God speaking to Solomon. When one looks at the way Solomon started, one would expect the Lord's last word to Solomon to have been one of joy. Instead the last word that Solomon received from the Lord was one of judgment. It was one of condemnation rather than commendation. It was one of disappointment rather than delight. It was one about decrease rather than increase. It was one of wrath rather than one of welcome. Solomon's mistake was that he forgot that the key to his blessings was a "til death do us part" expectation and commandment from God. When God spoke to Solomon, God promised that Solomon's fortune would last as long as Solomon walked in the ways of the Lord as his father David had done. David was far from perfect to be true, but David had a heart that was true to God. God knew that no matter what happened in David's life or what David did or did not do, God could count on David. The ultimate difference between David and his son Solomon was that David had a "til death do us part" relationship with God, and Solomon did not. No matter what chapter David may have been in at any given moment in his life, David's heart stayed with God.

If we would have life long prosperity and joy and if our desire is that our latter days be greater than our former days, then stay with God. In all our ups and downs, our risings and our fallings, stay with God. If we stay with God "til death do us part," then God will raise us from what is supposed to be our death to greater glory. Hear the last words of the Lord Jesus as he hung on the cross, "Father into your hands I commend my spirit. (Luke 23: 46)" Because he stayed with God till death separated them, what was supposed to be separation only became transformation into a greater and victorious Christ who now lives and reigns as King of Kings, and Lord of Lords. When we stay with God 'til death parts us, then God will stay with us even in death when we can no longer hold on to Him. Paul put it like this, "I am persuaded that neither death nor life, nor angels, nor rulers, not things present, nor things to come, no powers, nor height, not depth, not anything else in all creation, will be able to separate us from the love of God in Christ Jesus our Lord. (Romans 8: 38-39)" Therefore stay with God!

OTHER RESOURCES BY WILLIAM D. WATLEY:

TITLE	PRICE	QUANTITY
Preparing Joshua	$12.00	
Are You The One?	$10.00	
Bring the Full Tithe	$12.00	
Exalting the Names of Jesus	$10.00	
From Mess to Miracles	$12.00	
God Wants You to Grow How to Live Beyond Your Limitations	$14.00	
Less Than Tipping, Questions About Tithing	1- 99 $2.50 100-499 $2.25 500-999 $2.00 1,000+ $1.75 Priced per copy	
Less Than Tipping, Twenty-five Reasons to Tithe	1- 99 $10.00 100-499 $9.50 500-999 $9.00 1,000+ $8.50 Priced per copy	
Preaching in Two Voices	$12.00	
Roots of Resistance	$17.00	
Sermons From The Black Pulpit	$12.00	
Sermons on Special Days	$12.00	
The African American Pulpit (Millennium Issue)	$10.00	
The African Presence in the Bible	$14.00	
You Have To Face It To Fix It	$13.00	
	Total Enclosed	

Shipping Charges: 1-3 books add $2.00, 4-6 books add $5.00, 6 or more up to 99 add $8.00, 100 or more books FREE shipping. Canadian residents add $2.50 more as priced above. Pamphlet prices 1-499 add $2.00 500-1000 add $4.00.

Date	
Name	
Address	

Please send this form to St. James AME Church, 588 Martin Luther Kig Boulevard, Newark, New Jersey 07102 Attention: Executive Assistant. Please allow 1 week for delivery.